FLOWERING TREES AND SHRUBS
IN COLOUR

Edited by
F B Stark, C B Link and E L Packer

Galley Press

Contents

3 Trees and shrubs in the history of gardens
5 The use of trees and shrubs
5 Trees
5 Paths and roads
6 Shrubs
6 Hedges
7 Shrubs for the rock garden
7 Propagation, planting and culture
7 Propagation by seed
8 Vegetative propagation
9 Nursery operations
9 Planting
10 Culture
10 Prevention and cure of damage to trees
11 Problems
    Climatic damage
    Human action
    Insect attacks
    Diseases
13 Glossary
16 Index of plants mentioned
17 The conifers
29 Broadleaved trees
50 Flowering shrubs
58 Foliage shrubs
63 Fruiting shrubs

Picture Credits: C. Mariorossi: cover; Archivio I.G.D.A.: 3, 4, 20, 28, 29, 32, 33, 34, 39, 41, 45, 46, 52, 54, 57, 58, 62, 88, 112, 113; M. Bavestrelli: 17, 31, 69, 111, 139; C. Bevilacqua: 24, 51, 53, 63, 81, 115, 116, 118, 122, 123, 127, 135, 154, 162, 166; Bravo: 73; E.P.S.: 1, 23, 25, 38, 48, 74, 82, 83, 84, 85, 91, 92, 93, 97, 98, 103, 106, 109, 110, 126, 143, 144, 146, 147, 149, 150, 155, 158, 172; R. Longo: 77, 99, 105, 121, 125, 140, 141; A. Margiocco: 37; P. Martini: 124, 161; G. P. Mondino: 5, 16, 19, 21, 22, 27, 30, 35, 40, 42, 43, 44, 47, 49, 50, 55, 56, 60, 65, 68, 70, 71, 72, 75, 79, 87, 89, 94, 101, 107, 108, 114, 117, 119, 142, 148, 153, 159, 160, 163, 164, 165, 168, 169, 170, 173; P 2: 61, 78, 90, 128, 129, 130, 131, 132, 133, 134, 136, 137, 138, 145, 151, 152, 171; M. Pedone: 80. 96. 156. 157, 167; A. Sella: 9, 10, 11, 13, 15; G. Tomsich: 100, 104; S. Viola: 64, 66, 86, 102, 120.

Adapted from the Italian of Gian Paolo Mondino
Edited by Francis C. Stark, Conrad B. Link and Edwin Packer

© Orbis Publishing Limited, London 1974
© Istituto Geografico De Agostini, Novara 1969
Published in this edition 1981 by
Galley Press, an imprint of W H Smith and Son Limited
Registered No. 237811 England
Trading as WHS Distributors,
St John's House, East Street,
Leicester, LE1 6NE

Printed in Italy by New Interlitho, Milan
ISBN 0-86136-008-7

Trees and shrubs in the history of gardens

Trees have always held a fascination for man. Why this should be is a matter for conjecture. They impress with their strength and they display an infinite variety of shapes, forms and habits of growth. They provide a link with the past. And there are other reasons why man values the presence of trees. For many thousands of years they have provided him with timber for housing, furniture and fencing, for ships and implements, and for the manufacture of all kinds of useful and ornamental objects.

Throughout history they have played a part in man's religious life as the sacred groves of the Greeks, the Romans, the Gauls, and the Germans attest. In Britain forests of huge oaks were revered and protected by the Druids before the Roman invasion. Unfortunately most of the ancient oaks in Britain have disappeared but there are still protected groves of venerable yews and beeches. The Greeks consecrated the oak to their god Jupiter; the tree was also sacred to the Celtic people, as well as to the Germans who dedicated it to Thor. That these beliefs persisted as superstitions even with the advent of Christianity is shown by a decree of Charlemagne of 789 A.D. (which remained unobserved) ordering the cutting of the sacred woods, and by the numerous decrees, promulgated by Councils in Germany and Britain until the thirteenth century, against those who practised divination beneath the trees. The fact that modern man also finds something esoteric and noble in trees is demonstrated by our planting of trees in parks or forests as living memorials to those killed in war.

In the brief historical introduction that follows, the development of landscape architecture is described, and the role played in various epochs by trees and shrubs—which are the basic, coordinating elements of gardens—will be noted.

From antiquity we have evidence of Egyptian gardens with a regular design, of the Hanging Gardens of Babylon with straight paths, of the more natural Greek gardens with tree groves and flower beds. We know more about Roman gardens based on their representation in mosaics, and by archaeological finds and writings. Their centre was usually a small piazza with fountains, crisscrossed by rectilinear paths like the streets of their cities.

Flanking the lanes of cypresses, pines, oaks, palms, olives and lindens were hedges of rosemary, myrtle and box with clumps of holly and laurel; here and there were such decorative elements as vases, statues, small temples, colonnades and fountains. Gardeners pruned shrubs into the most varied topiary forms, sometimes transforming them into works of art.

Many centuries before Christ the Chinese garden with its irregular design was well developed, and descriptions of it have come to us with examples handed down from imperial and monastic gardens. The elements of the garden were rather complex; a skilful use was made of water, and thought was given to the disposition of buildings, rocks, grottoes, hills and panoramas so that the vistas were diversified—all of which contributed to the enchantment of the view and stirred the imagination. The trees and shrubs most often used were the flowering cherries, dwarf maples, magnolias, camelias, bamboo and hydrangeas.

The Japanese garden is influenced by the Chinese; while simple in structure, it is often symbolic of man's emotions. Gardens of dwarf firs are typical of this form.

In the Moslem garden, of which eloquent testimony remains in the Alhambra at Granada, great importance was attached to water which was used not only for aesthetic purposes but also to moderate the temperature in the courtyards. The luxurious garden of the Generalife still exists.

During the Middle Ages, with the difficulties and insecurity of the times, gardens were maintained inside the walls of castles and monasteries and became functional with plantings of fruits and vegetables. A creation of the Renaissance is the Italian garden, wherein man bent nature to his ends, adapting the landscape to the new spirit of the times. These gardens are notable for a geometrical rigidity of design, a heritage of ancient Rome. The Florentine garden of the fifteenth century, situated on the plain, was characterized by the evergreen hedges defining formal beds and the use of shrubs, as well as trees with even tops, to form various designs. The hedges, the vines on the pergolas, the shrubs outlining the mazes and the trees with high trunks were pruned; trees formed groups with a constructive purpose. The garden was embellished with statues, vases,

4

sarcophagi (a relic of Roman gardens), fountains and seats. In the sixteenth century, Italian gardens took on a more ornamental character; an important innovation was their use to complement the home in the countryside.

In the Roman garden of the sixteenth century, constructed on a slope, these elements remained but they were set picturesquely on terraces, each level connected to the others by flights of stairs; here water acquired greater decorative importance in fountains, streams and waterfalls. In the seventeenth century the baroque elements were accentuated and greater importance was given to construction, using fountains, nymphs, grottoes, and colonnades.

The rigid scheme of the Italian garden was taken and made more elaborate in the French garden, designed on rolling terrain, particularly through the work of Le Notre (1613–1700) in which the important element of perspective was introduced. Here trees and groves were kept distant from buildings to give a broad sweep to the panorama, while in the foreground were placed flower beds, lawns, beds of shrubs and pools of water with statues and fountains.

The central walk, intersected by side paths, was laid out on the long axis, with groves interposed. The beds often contained plants that could be trimmed into geometrical forms; the same principle was applied in the case of the vines, hedges and mazes. The buildings in the garden took the form of informal or formal pavilions. The French garden spread to Germany, Austria and Italy during the

eighteenth century; in the latter country it became popular in regions less influenced by the Italian school.

The English garden, pictorial or natural, was a romantic reaction to the cold academism of earlier styles; influenced by Chinese gardens, it sought to relate to the surrounding countryside. The guiding principle of this garden was no longer the imposition of artificiality but a blending with nature, suitably proportioned with finishing touches and embellishments. Symmetry, straight lines and pruning were thus abandoned. Great importance was given to well cared for carpets of grass and curving paths, and to water reproducing natural springs, brooks and lakes. Specimen trees were emphasized, and groves were of an irregular shape, each usually composed of a single species. In these gardens a great number of exotic plants, at that time only recently discovered, were introduced.

In the nineteenth century eclecticism triumphed in garden design as it did in architecture without, however, often attaining a valid artistic mix. In this period, orangeries and conservatories, already in existence in the eighteenth century, became widespread.

In the present century there has been an increase in the number of public gardens in cities and a decrease in private gardens. Gardens once were the privilege of a few; today they perform a social function in being accessible to all citizens and especially to children. They are important at a time like today when city life is becoming more and more

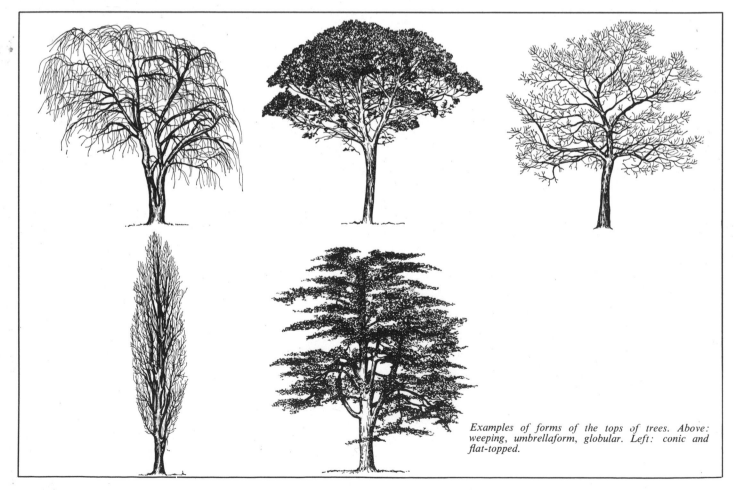

Examples of forms of the tops of trees. Above: weeping, umbrellaform, globular. Left: conic and flat-topped.

artificial. In addition to their aesthetic value, the function performed by trees and plants—that of ameliorating the polluted air of the urban conglomeration—is of importance to health. In recent decades we have witnessed a deterioration of the environment due to highway construction, industrialization and housing, and the balance should be redressed.

The use of trees and shrubs

Trees and shrubs form the backbone of the garden; thus their choice and setting are of the greatest importance. In general terms, these woody plants must be suited to the surroundings, not only to avoid damage from the weather, but also so as not to introduce plants that do not blend well with the landscape. The distinction between trees and shrubs is not always clear cut, because species of trees which are large under normal conditions become shrubs when growing near the altitudinal or latitudinal limits of the species. So the aspen can be found 100 feet tall at a low altitude but is no more than a 4 feet shrub-size in the high Rocky Mountains. The form, not the size, is the deciding feature.

To make the design stand out, trees and shrubs should, if possible, leave a vista of the surrounding countryside in order to give a background that, visually and aesthetically, seems to spread from the garden to the horizon, creating the illusion of greater breathing space. When a large park is planned, it is best to leave the entrance free and facing the view, with a broad carpet of grass directly in front and with those trees of great height in the distance. In level areas one can give the impression of a more rolling landscape by alternating tall groups of plants with shorter ones. On the other hand, if the ground already has considerable slope, this may be softened visually by the use of the shorter plants on the heights and the taller trees on the lower sites.

The choice of plants depends on their particular characteristics; a broadleaf gives shade in hot weather but is bare in winter, while conifers give little shade but keep their ornamental effect in winter. With deciduous types, however, the fine web of the branches and the particular effect of an interesting bark, no longer hidden by leaves, can become aesthetically appealing during winter. The relationship between trees and shrubs must be undertaken with care to avoid extreme contrasts of colour and form, or a complete lack of contrast. Thus plants of a particular form, towering or weeping, should be kept apart, while collections of shrubs (for example, dwarf firs, or those with coloured tops) may be grouped. It is also very important to choose species with an eye to their future development; thus, if a garden is of limited size, it should be designed for plants of restrained height to achieve a good aesthetic effect with time. Finally, it is necessary to restrict the choice to a certain number of species for planting and grouping, so that you do not overload the garden with so many kinds as to make it resemble a botanical garden.

Trees

Trees may be set out individually as specimens or in groups, to create groves and green arches, to form curtains and paths. In the first case we are dealing in general with a tree of great stature (although not always) which has aesthetic characteristics that attract the eye to its particular shape, the form or colour of the bark, the shape and colour of the leaves, the flowers, or the fruit, or its appearance in a particular season. The thickets or groups, composed of trees of lesser stature, can serve as protection to delicate plants or flower beds, to prepare the eye for changes of view, to give tones of colour, to give movement to areas that otherwise would be monotonous, and to act as screens.

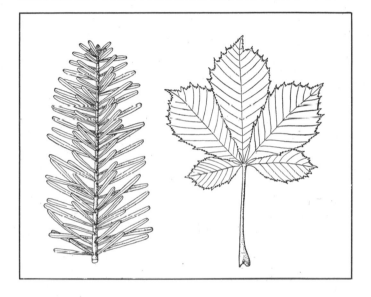

Examples of needle leaves (conifer) at left, and broadleaves.

To form groves, the preference will doubtless be given to plants native to the region or perhaps, to obtain an effect in shorter time, to some rapidly growing conifer. The green "vaults" or arches—decorative covered paths or roads that require considerable maintenance—are excellent for the entrances to large gardens. They must be created with trees that permit heavy pruning. If maximum height is desired, the choice may be made from among plane trees, elms, horse chestnuts and lindens; if a lower height is wanted, the hornbeam is preferred. Screening plants are, in practice, high hedges, and these are discussed later.

Paths and roads

Whether in the urban or the non-urban landscape, lanes of tall trees add an aesthetic note. There has recently been much discussion over the propriety of planting trees outside cities because of the disadvantages they create for high-speed automobile traffic on narrow winding roads. In cities, certainly, trees beautify, provide shade, and improve the air in that plants, by photosynthesis, take in carbon dioxide, the waste of human respiration and of combustion, and return oxygen to the air. In addition, the broadleaved trees regulate the temperature of a restricted atmosphere by the emission of water vapour and the absorption of heat.

History gives us examples of urban plantings as far back as Roman days, when the streets of the patricians were embellished with them. In the Middle Ages and later there is no mention of lanes until 1616, when at the insistence of Marie de Medici a lane of elms was planted at the Cours-la-Reine in Paris. In 1650, a lane of lindens and walnuts was planted in Berlin. In France, the planting of trees along city streets became general during the First Empire.

The distance of trees from the front of dwellings and from the edge of the street should be sufficient to ensure that drastic or too frequent pruning will not be required. The proper spacing of trees along the rows and their position, if they are set in parallel rows, is very important. For trees that grow to 75 feet, the spacing should be about 40 feet; for those 40 feet high, 27 feet; for those 20 feet high, 12 feet, and so on—interpolating for intermediate heights and increasing the distance in proportion if there is more than one row. In this instance the trees can be set out in squares, to form rows in two directions, or at the points of equilateral triangles, forming rows in three directions. If shade is desired quickly, trees may be placed at half distance, every other one being removed later to allow for natural growth.

The spacing of trees depends also on the form assumed by their tops and on their shape; towering trees with soaring branches, such as the Lombardy poplar, have a close-gathered head and so may be planted more closely than indicated above.

In the selection of species it is wise to keep in mind the climatic and soil requirements. If, as is usual, shade is wanted, one must plant broadleaved trees with a broad, dense top (plane trees, elms, maples, lindens, horse chestnut, etc.). If only a particular aesthetic effect is desired, one will plant conifers or such flowering trees and shrubs as red bud, mimosa, *Paulownia*, apple, plum, magnolia, crape-myrtle, or those with ornamental fruit (e.g. *Pyracantha*).

Trees that are heavily scented when in bloom can be troublesome to some persons as can the unpleasant odour coming from the leaves of the ailanthus and the fruit of the ginkgo.

Of the dangers besetting trees on city streets, some are almost specific to the kind of tree. Others are due to such extraneous factors as gas leaks, deposits of dust, or poisonous gases in the atmosphere. With underground gas leaks the roots become asphyxiated, and when this happens the soil must be thoroughly aerated before replanting. Dust and gas in the air physically obstruct the stomata at first, next "burning" the leaves. Some conifers are particularly susceptible to air pollutants. The tips of their needles turn reddish-brown and wither. Among broadleaved trees the chestnut, the linden and the elm are susceptible because of their rough or hairy leaves; those with smooth leaves or leaves that move easily in the breeze are less harmed.

Shrubs

The choice of shrubs ranges over a great number of plants of the most diverse requirements and ornamental qualities. There are three main categories: those for flowers, those for fruit and those for foliage. Bear in mind, however, that there are no strict lines between them.

The first group which stand out better in masses against a grassy background, provide us with a good selection that will keep the garden in flower the whole summer, with some actual winter bloom if the site has good exposure (such as *Chimonanthus fragrans*, *Hamamelis mollis*, *Erica carnea*). Beginning with the earliest kinds gradually coming into bloom in spring, we have forsythia and *Chaenomeles japonica*, then various viburnums, spirea and dogwood (the splendid *Cornus florida*), azaleas, rhododendrons, lilacs, *Deutzia*, mock orange and hawthorn.

These are followed by the summer flowering of *Buddleia*, *Ceanothus*, *Hibiscus*, some spireas and others. Among the shrubs that flower at the same time, one should give consideration to the location of diverse types, so their colours do not clash but create a harmonious setting (this is especially important for rhododendrons).

Fruit also gives a bright note to shrubs, especially if it persists over winter, as with *Pyracantha*, *Contoneaster* and some hollies.

Hedges

The functions of hedges in the garden are manifold, and these must be discussed at some length when dealing with suitable species. Hedges, especially of evergreens, had their greatest success in the Renaissance and the sixteenth and seventeenth centuries, as true architectural elements of the Italian garden and, later, of the French garden. Today, hedges (high screens or low plantings) are used to outline the limits of the property, to divide the garden into parts, to screen walls that disrupt the setting and to protect against wind.

Plants suitable for hedges are mostly of shrubby growth; they should have dense foliage and be able to tolerate pruning. Choice should be made with ecological criteria in mind; some of these plants tolerate shade well, others want more sun, and still others must be used only in sheltered positions not too cold in winter. Insofar as possible, evergreens are chosen so that the screen is maintained throughout the year. The choice of species is long and certainly is not exhausted by the examples that follow: the very hardy privet; the low but ornamental barberry, *Berberis Thunbergii*; the numerous *Cotoneasters*; the *Pyracanthas*, ornamental in fruit and foliage; *Chaenomeles japonica*; *Elaeagnus pungens*; laurel; spirea; hibiscus; box, rather elegant, but slow-growing; holly; and cherry laurel. For high hedges (screens) choose from taller species such as hornbeam, Arizona cypress, yew, arborvitae, and holm oak. Among plants suited only to the warmest maritime localities of southern England, or to the greenhouse, choose from *Pittosporum*, myrtle, rosemary, oleander, croton, arbutus, holm oaks, laurel, and viburnum—all evergreen. Hardy varieties of some of these can be obtained.

If an impassable hedge is desired, choose spiny plants such as hawthorn, *Citrus trifoliata*, and *Maclura pomifera* or, for warmer areas, Christ's thorn (*Paliurus spina-Christi*). After the planting of hedges, it is necessary to cut back the tops to encourage lateral branches and to thicken foliage, particularly at the base (this is done two or three times a year). When the hedge is finally shaped, it is sheared to keep it attractive, the frequency depending on the species and its growth rate.

Shrubs for the rock garden

Although the majority of plants grown in the rock garden are herbaceous or somewhat bushy, it is good to introduce some shrubs to make the total setting livelier. The rock garden seems ready-made for the limited space we have today for our gardens, and its lack of popularity may be that it is difficult to construct.

The rock garden is an arrangement of rocks (siliceous or calcareous according to the requirements of the plants one wants to grow), among the clefts of which are placed plants indigenous to rocky surroundings and primarily from the mountains.

The choice of woody plants for this purpose are those of limited development and slow growth. They must not give too much shade to herbaceous plants, nor should they make the environment unnatural; the limited size of most rock gardens rules out large-growing types, which, of course, would not find conditions suitable in the rock clefts, pockets of earth and small terraces.

Suitable shrubby plants may be found among the natural flora (Mugo pine, *Erica carnea*, the azaleas), and some conifers have wonderful shapes suited to this purpose, including *Chamaecyparis*, with its diverse species and numerous cultivars, cone-shaped, globular, or weeping in habit, and dense, compact top, often of varied colours. Among these are: *Chamaecyparis obtusa* var. *ericoides*, purple in winter; *C. obtusa* var. *nana*; *C. obtusa* var. *pygmaea*, bronze-green; and *C. obtusa* var. *tetragona*, with golden, mosslike foliage.

Another group of conifers suited to rock gardens is the junipers, of rather variable shape. *Picea Abies*, too, the common spruce used as Christmas trees, has various cultivars useful here, as do the arborvitae. The dwarf yew may be used for shaded slopes and northern exposures. Among the broadleaved evergreens are some rhododendrons; *Cistus* (only for sheltered positions); *Berberis buxifolia*, with orange flowers and dark blue berries; and the various *Cotoneasters*. Among deciduous broadleaves, *Cytisus* hybrids, various brooms, some daphnes and *Helianthemum*, some *Ceanothus*, *Hypericum calycinum*, and *Potentilla fruticosa* are recommended.

Propagation, planting, and culture

The propagation of plants is the basis of the nursery industry; the techniques are being refined with time, aided in recent years by artificial illumination, water mists in greenhouses, low-volume irrigation, mechanical transplanters, the use of growth regulators, insecticides, fungicides and herbicides.

Propagation is fundamentally of two types: sexual (by seed) and asexual (or vegetative) including division, layering, air layering, cuttings and grafting.

Propagation by seed

The specimens that result from the propagation of plants by seed are generally very vigorous, but the method is limited to the reproduction of species in which the desired characters do not vary and breed true, and are transmitted genetically. Some characters are reproduced only by vegetative means.

Male and female cells, known as gametes, in the cell are responsible for the reproductive process; the female developing to produce the new plant when given the impetus by the male.

After harvest, seeds are usually sown in sand or a soil mixture. Some species, however, must spend the winter in the ground to permit the seed to truly ripen; the same result may be obtained by refrigerating the seeds in a moist peat moss medium until growth begins, after which they should be planted in soil. Certain seeds with a hard shell must be scarified before planting. Other seeds, such as mimosa and *Acer palmatum*, are soaked in warm water before sowing to ensure rapid germination.

Regarding the soil medium for the seedlings, a loamy mixture is best to get good root development. The soil should be easy to till after rain, and must be well-drained to prevent root rot. Irrigation must be provided as well as a suitable system for eliminating excess water.

Seeds are sown in spring, when the soil warms suitably, usually in rows to simplify weeding; depth is in relation to the size of the seeds—in general a depth 5 times the diameter except for very large seeds. Very small seeds, such as those of rhododendrons, should not be covered with soil, or only lightly. If broadcast sowing must be done, choose days without wind and mix small seeds with sand or other material to make sowing more uniform. The seedlings must be given water and shade, and diseases, insects and weeds must be controlled. Weeding is done by hand, by mechanical implements (tillers, motorized cultivators), or by chemical means (herbicides or weed killers)—but is unnecessary if sowing is in sterilized soil. After some months it is necessary to transplant the seedlings to provide more space for the plants and to let the roots develop. Some care must be taken in digging the plants to ensure that the roots are not injured or allowed to get dry. At this time only the better seedlings are chosen.

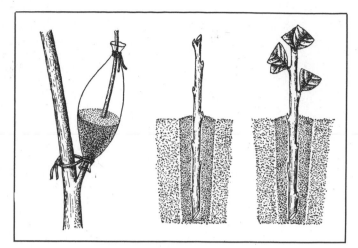

Vegetative reproduction; (from left), air layering, hardwood cutting, softwood cutting.

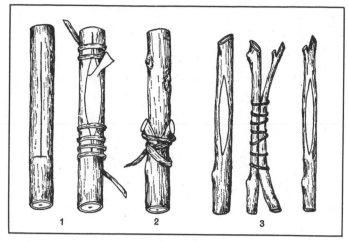

Grafting: (1) budding; (2) cleft graft; (3) approach graft.

Vegetative propagation

Division is a simple method but is not used in large-scale operations. It is limited to shrubs that produce rooted side shoots. Examples of this are *Kerria japonica*, *Hypericum calycinum*, *Rhus typhina*, *Chaenomeles japonica*, *Deutzia*, *Philadelphus*, bamboo, heather, and some forms of spirea. The operation is performed by taking up plants and dividing them. This should be carried out in spring for foliage plants or those with late bloom, in autumn for those with early spring bloom, and at the beginning of growth in the spring for bamboo. The individual specimens are treated like young plants.

Shrubs with pliant branches, such as rhododendrons and magnolias, may be propagated by layering; that is, by bending a branch and pegging it into the ground after having girdled it slightly or after removing the bark. The tip of the shoot must be kept erect. With plants of long and very flexible branches, such as honeysuckle, each branch may go into and out of the earth several times, yielding more plants. Although this is a slow process (it may take two, three or more years before the offspring can be separated from the mother plant), it is a sure type of propagation, applicable to plants of particular value.

For air layering, moist sphagnum is placed around a girdled branch and wrapped with a piece of plastic. This ancient method, of Chinese origin, must have the medium kept constantly moist, which is easy when polyethylene is used. Production of roots is enhanced by the use of a rooting hormone on the surface of the branch before applying the sphagnum. Wind breakage is averted by fixing the package with splints. From the callus of the scar the roots emerge; when this occurs, the rooted branch is cut off and planted in a pot until the following spring. Spring is the most appropriate time of the year for air layering to obtain plants by early autumn. This is, however, a slow and laborious method, used especially for certain conifers and delicate shrubs.

Propagation by cuttings is the most common method of vegetative reproduction since the vegetative characteristics are reproduced. The method is economical as well, permitting an easy and rapid multiplication of a large quantity of plants. In the case of trees and shrubs, branches are usually placed in the medium for rooting; root cuttings are used of such genera as *Paulowia* and *Rhus*.

Cuttings may be of soft or green wood taken during summer, or of hard, mature wood taken in winter. Softwood cuttings are taken from June to September, from that year's growth; 2 to 6-inch pieces of branch are cut below a node, the lower leaves are removed, and the cuttings planted in sand, under glass, or in a humid greenhouse. The roots are formed when new growth is observed and the rooted cutting may then be transplanted. This method has a good success rate for most deciduous shrubs. Pines and such evergreens as *Aucuba*, camelia, oleander, box, privet, and euonymus are propagated in late summer, with partially mature wood.

Cuttings of hard, or mature wood, are made 6 to 12 inches long from the same year's growth, from November to February. They are sometimes taken with a "spur" of second year wood, which enhances rooting. They are placed in the sand with only one or two buds exposed. *Philadelphus*, *Deutzia*, *Forsythia*, *Spiraea*, *Tamarix*, *Cornus*, *Salix*, and various roses are propagated in this fashion.

Root cuttings are made of sections of roots and planted vertically in pots with the portion that was closest to the stem placed at the top. Rooting is improved by continuous mist.

Grafting is the intimate union of the tissues of two related plants, one of which has the root system (the stock) and the other, the graft (scion). For the scion a portion of a branch or a single leaf bud may be used; these are called, respectively, *grafting* and *budding*. These methods are used when cuttings take root with difficulty and with those plants whose characteristics do not come true from seed.

The practice is ancient; the Greeks knew budding, stem grafting, and crown grafting. The union of the two parts is effected by the two meristematic tissues, the *phellogen*, which produces bark on the outside and the cortical parenchyma on the inside, and the *cambium*, which generates the inner bark and the wood. It is necessary that stock and scion be related; the relationship is closest among varieties of the same species and between species of the same genus. Frequently, genera belonging to the same family (as between privet and lilac) may be grafted satisfactorily.

The cut must be smooth (use grafting knives that are well sharpened), and the surfaces must be clean. Besides the principal aim of propagation, grafting permits substituting one variety for another, growing a plant in soil not suited to it, obtaining greater vigour in the grafted plant, or dwarfing by the use of a weaker stock.

The forms of grafts are boundless, but those most used in gardening are: *approach grafts*, made by closely linking two stems after removing the bark at the point of contact—this is done for propagating mimosa; *cleft grafting*, done by shaping the scion like the mouthpiece of a flute and inserting it into a cleft of the stock; and *budding*, done by inserting a stem bud into a cut made T-shaped or in the form of a cross in the stock, the method used for garden roses.

Formerly, grafts were bound with raffia or wool thread; now there is widespread use of rubber bands, self-adhering gums, and adhesive tape. Bud grafts should be covered with mastic gum or dipped in paraffin to prevent drying and the growth of mould on the exposed surface.

The best time for budding is when the plant sap is most active; then the bark peels easily. Grafting is usually done towards the end of winter before plant growth begins. For slow-growing plants the union may take from 6 to 8 weeks. There are also types of root grafting: wisteria and rhododendrons are propagated in this way with ease; the union of stem and root occurs naturally.

Nursery operations

Plants obtained from seed or by vegetative reproduction, after having rooted, are "lined-out" in nursery beds with enough space for good development and root spread. Watering in the summer will be necessary, although it need be done only sparingly in the case of firs. One should not prune roots or branches of firs but they may be shortened in some broadleaved trees by removing one of the occasional double heads or encouraging a side branch to become the leader if the latter is gone. During this stay in the nursery, the development of the branches ("framework") begins that will in time produce a crown of foliage.

The best time for transplanting from the nursery is when the plant is dormant. Particular caution must be observed in the case of evergreens (especially firs), since they transpire uninterruptedly; one should therefore avoid periods of freezing or windy weather. To facilitate the transport of developed specimens of evergreens and firs, the ball of soil around the roots is usually wrapped in burlap.

Planting

As far as possible (especially in heavy soil) it is wise to till the soil well, months in advance, from 16 to 20 inches deep in what are to be permanent sites for trees so that frost, sun, and rain will make the soil loose and crumbly, permitting good circulation of air and water. In this operation subsoil, low in organic matter, should not be mixed with the topsoil.

When planting in poor soil, large holes are dug and replaced with good soil. Manure and peat can be incorporated. Wet soil should have a drainage layer of gravel at the bottom of the hole or a system of porous pipes to carry off water.

The quality and vigour of plants set out are related to their early growth; it is therefore important to make a wise choice of material for planting. Plants should have a trunk of good diameter and a balance between root system and top. It is preferable that the soil of the nursery bed and that of the permanent site be of a similar nature. The same may be said of the climate, although the climate of the nursery bed should be a little harsher, yielding hardier plants.

Holes should be large enough to allow a great deal of loose soil to be applied to the roots (5 to 6 feet wide and 3 feet deep). Autumn planting gives the best guarantee of success, except in the case of evergreens with a ball of earth which are planted in late winter, and palms which should be transplanted in June or July.

The roots must not be placed in contact with fertilizer. Suitable spacing is of great importance; this depends on the height the plant can attain, its habits (sun-loving or shade-loving), and the aesthetic effect sought. In digging holes for planting, it is better to keep subsoil separate from topsoil and to put the latter in contact with the roots. If immediate planting is not possible, the plants are "heeled in", with the roots in a trench and covered with earth. If plants have been partly frozen in transit, they must be thawed slowly in a sheltered spot; on the other hand, if the plants have been crowded close together in warm weather and overheated (by warmth generated through transpiration), they must be given air and moisture at once.

Plants should be set at the same depth they grow in the nursery. Burlap around the root ball should be loosely cut at the top, to free the roots, but not removed.

After planting it is almost always essential to keep the plant upright with a stake, in order to prevent it from being bent by winds and to keep the roots from being displaced. The stakes should be set parallel to the trunk, supporting it with elastic bands or metal wires covered with rubber to avoid injuring the bark. Slanting supports may be wires or poles.

Watering will be necessary immediately after planting. For large palms, water should be allowed to run from a hose for several days in succession at the base of the plant. Often the trunks are protected by metal grills, screen wire, thorny branches, etc., so they will not be displaced or damaged.

When very large specimens are to be transplanted, the root ball is made well ahead of time by digging a trench at some distance around the base of the tree and filling the trench with organic materials, such as peat moss. Transplanting can be done about six months later.

Digging and transporting trees are difficult procedures because of the risk of harming the branches or the bark, especially with conifers. On the other hand, plane trees with a circumference of more than five feet, with all branches removed, may be planted in midsummer and then take good hold, forming a new top in a few years.

Culture

If there is a failure among trees planted for hedgerows or screens the gap should be filled as soon as possible. Larger trees may have to be used to keep pace with those already planted.

Care taken after planting consists of watering, cultivation, fertilizing, adjustment of the supports, trimming, and protection from cold and snow.

Cultivation consists of light hoeing of the layer of earth above the roots to break the crust that may be formed in tamping the soil. In the spring, chemical fertilizers are hoed shallowly into the earth. In both operations caution must be employed not to injure the roots, especially those of firs which grow new ones with difficulty. The binding of the supports must be inspected from time to time to make sure there is no danger of girdling the trunk.

Pruning may be needed to remove dead or diseased branches or suckers, to reinvigorate declining deciduous trees, to trim branches broken by snow or wind, to even the top, to increase height, to thin the trees (as, for example, when they are too close to electric power lines), and to shape screens and hedges. The cuts must be made with sharp tools flush with the trunk—without, however, damaging the bark.

There are many hindrances to free growth of street trees: trimming and other provisions made for the sake of safety (ensuring that the wind does not break off heavy branches, for example), the elimination of screens on public lighting, the danger of contact with overhead electric lines, too much shade, and the desire to give artificial shapes to the top.

Although pruning is needed especially by deciduous trees, it may be useful on certain conifers, such as Arizona cypress which if not trimmed loses its compact top, and boxwood and arborvitae when artificial shapes are wanted. The extent of pruning must be diversified according to the tolerance of the various kinds to this treatment.

If a given species does not tolerate drastic pruning, it is necessary to prune it lightly and more often. A particular and most specialized type of pruning is that by which so-called dwarf (or Bonsai) plants are achieved.

Pruning of flowering shrubs must be varied according to whether blooms appear on new growth or that of the preceding year. In the first case (as in *Philadelphus*, *Deutzia*, *Diervilla*, *Hydrangea*), in which flowering occurs in summer on new growth, pruning may be done until winter. In the second case one should wait until flowering is over (e.g., for *Forsythia* and *Jasminum nudiflorum*) so that new shoots for next year's bloom may then develop.

The most appropriate season for pruning is generally near end of winter, just before new vegetative growth begins. Evergreen species susceptible to frost should not be trimmed early, because their resistance to low temperatures is associated with the storing up of reserve substances that would be removed by pruning.

During heavy snows, especially if they are wet, broken branches of evergreens are avoided by shaking their tops and removing the weight of snow. Valuable or small plants are usually protected from cold, and especially from frost, with a protective covering of the trunk or of the entire plant, at least in their early years.

Prevention and cure of damage to trees

There are many causes of damage to trees; some of these, however, may be prevented. In case of construction near trees, they may be protected by a temporary fence, while in other cases adequate permanent defence can be provided to keep transient vehicles from coming too close (for example, in parking areas). Damage from cold (e.g., splitting from the action of frost) can be avoided by binding the trunks of delicate specimens with burlap. Specific insecticides will avoid or reduce the damage from insects.

When a branch is pruned, especially if it is large, the cut must be made properly without wounding the bark or leaving a stump. In any case, the cut must be smooth, clean, without rough edges, and slanted so that rainwater will run off. The cut surfaces are treated with preservatives such as asphalt paint or tar to prevent disease infection.

A frequent need in old specimens is the treatment of trunks hollowed by wood fungi, in general progressing from the bottom to the top. To restore strength to the weakened plant, it is first necessary to remove all of the decayed wood until live tissue is reached, then to disinfect and close the hole to keep other harmful organisms, that like humidity, from infesting it. The filling of large cavities is expensive and also very difficult because material with the same characteristics of expansion and contraction as wood do not exist. Mortar, cement, blocks of treated wood, mixtures of asphalt and sawdust, and magnesite are used for this purpose.

Large metal rings may be inserted in the cavity to reinforce the tree and to give better anchor to the filling material. The ring is kept in a narrow circumference relative to that of the trunk in order to permit it, if possible, to be filled with new tissue closing the wound. If there are only splits or soft wounds on the trunk, the edges of the wound are kept in place by metal clasps and a movable ring. These are also used, along with a metal stay rod, itself adjustable, to keep forked branches from growing further apart and splitting.

If the level of the terrain must be lowered, the level of that around the tree must be maintained by constructing a retaining wall. On the other hand, when the level of the terrain must be raised to ensure that the roots continue to be furnished with the normal amount of oxygen, the base of the tree must be kept free by creation of a well with dry walls around it. In addition a drainage layer of gravel, or, better still, porous drainage pipes set vertically and horizontally

A fungus harmful to woody plants: the honey mushroom (Armillariella mellea).

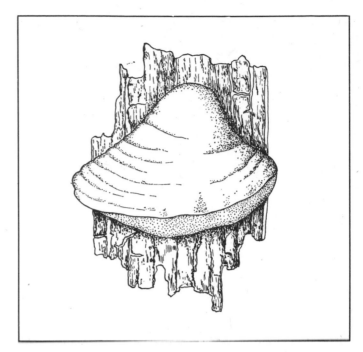

Another fungus that can cause the death of a tree; this appears as a flat surface or a clod attached to the trunk. Species of this sort are of the genera Fomes, Polyporus, Ganoderma, *etc.*

must be positioned beneath soil placed over the roots.

Lightning damage to trees does not usually occur when their whole surface is moist, since the discharge runs down along the trunk; but if the tree is struck at the beginning of a storm when the bark is still dry, the bark acts as an insulator, and the charge usually follows the cambium, killing it partially or entirely. Valuable specimens, especially if isolated and very tall, may be protected by lightning rods linked to the soil somewhat distant from the trunk.

Problems

The causes of damage or death to trees may be classified as climatic, human, insect, or due to diseases.

Climatic damage
Every plant has particular requirements in regard to its surroundings; if these are not respected, we may have plants that will grow with difficulty or not at all—or even die, in cases of extreme dryness, heat, or frost, for example. Often the great trees struck by lightning in parks lose their tops, are stripped of bark, or even die in the course of time.

Wet snowfalls or accumulations of freezing rain can split branches; strong winds can break branches or uproot the trees. Frost can cause longitudinal splits, leaving ugly calluses around the wound.

Cold air currents constantly from one direction may destroy the symmetry by partially drying up the top; near the sea, damage may be the result of salt spray.

Drought causes leaf-fall, drying of the branches, and in extreme cases death of the plant, which cannot substitute water absorbed for that lost by transpiration. And excess water deprives the roots of necessary oxygen and death results.

Human action
Very often it is man, directly or indirectly even if involuntarily, who causes damage to trees. We have already mentioned that "strangulation" by girdling and too close planting of trees causes deformation of the trunks and lack of symmetry in the crown.

Impenetrable street surfaces (asphalt or concrete) hinder the access of air and water to the roots. The harm from adding or removing earth at the foot of the tree has already been noted; also, excavations, drainage, and movement of earth in the vicinity can destroy the equilibrium of water supply by changing the level of the water table. Such conditions are unsatisfactory for root growth.

The air holds in suspension smoke, dust, and poisonous gases from domestic heating, from vehicular discharge, and from various industrial activities—all of which are damaging to trees. The air is most polluted where population is concentrated. The escape of gas underground has already been mentioned.

Insect attacks
Insect damage can affect any part of the plant; damage varies according to method of feeding, the biological cycle, and the degree of insect infestation.

Chewing insects cause defoliation. The several species of the winter moth group provide the majority of foliage-feeding caterpillars that move in a series of loops and so are known as "loopers". They feed upon apple trees, oak, hawthorn and beech. The moths emerge from the soil from

November to March, dependent on the species, and the wingless female ascends the tree on foot. The winged male seeks her out and after mating she lays eggs in crevices on twigs. When the caterpillars hatch out they feed mainly on the leaves but may also attack flowers and fruit.

Sucking insects nourish themselves on the sap inside the cells; aphids and scale insects are among the most harmful. The former sometimes cover the plants with downy or waxy efflorescence (e.g., the white aphids of the pine and the beech). The scale insects are covered with small shields and often envelop Japanese euonymus and other ornamentals.

These insects may be controlled by using insecticides. Since recommended controls change from time to time, specific materials will not be suggested in this book.

Old, declining trees are often attacked by wood-eating insects which dig out their passageways inside the bark. To this group belong also the white pine weevils (genus *Pissodes*) which cause desiccation of young shoots of conifers. The cypress poplar is host to numerous borers; the tunnels from which the sawdust comes out must be filled with a material that will give off poisonous vapours.

Leaf-mining insects disfigure leaves by tunnelling passages.

Diseases

The fungi harmful to the living parts of a plant are called parasites; because of their small dimensions they must be studied under a microscope. In some instances they belong to the group of ordinary mushrooms. Attacks of fungi cannot always be combated, especially if the affected plants are of great size.

In attempting to classify the pathogenic fungi according to their mode of action, those that cause the death of seedlings (plants that have just sprouted), such as damping-off organisms, are dealt with first. Other diseases attack the leaves, producing desiccation and leaf-fall; of this type are the black spots of maple leaves.

Mildew is caused by fungi that live on the surface of leaves, making them appear to be sprinkled with a whitish powder; various species live on oaks, roses, hydrangeas and lilacs.

Cankers are abnormal proliferation of cortical tissue, with swelling and malformation.

Rusts are so-called because the spores that issue from the tissues are rust-coloured. There are many species of fungi that attack various kinds of pines, and to complete their life cycle need the presence of certain herbaceous or shrubby plants (e.g., the currant, which is necessary for the complete life cycle of white pine rust).

A very serious vascular disease of the elm is the Dutch elm disease, caused by *Ceratostomella ulmi*; the pores of the tissues become occluded and the tree dries out. There is no remedy other than the substitution of an infected tree by the Siberian elm, which is immune. In most cases, the major damage to old trees in parks is due to root rot and core rot. Often the death of a tree already hollowed out is due to its weakness and the beating of the wind.

Now follows a description of trees and shrubs suitable and decorative for gardens. The trees are classified in subdivisions of conifers and broadleaves, and the shrubs into flowering, leafy, and fruiting shrubs, according to the decorative effect of the bloom, the foliage or the fruit. For the genera or the families of plants with several species in use by horticulturalists, one among the representatives is completely described, with brief notes on other types worthy of interest. The list of plants has been arranged, as far as possible, in systematic order, although, in mentioning plants with related use, representatives of other families are sometimes included. Information on the morphology and cultivation of the species is also given.

87. **Perianth**—the calyx and corolla.
88. **Persistent**—remaining attached.
89. **Petal**—one member of the corolla.
90. **Petiole**—the supporting stalk of the leaf blade.
91. **Pinnate**—separate leaflets arranged along a leaf stalk.
92. **Pistil**—the female reproductive parts of a flower, comprised of the stigma, style, and ovary.
*93. **Pome**—a fleshy, indehiscent fruit, with a leathery endocarp surrounding the seed, e.g., the apple.
94. **Pseudobulb**—thickened bulblike structure on leaves of epiphytic orchids.
95. **Pubescent**—covered with short hairs; downy.
96. **Raceme**—an elongated, indeterminate flower cluster with each floret on a pedicel.
97. **Rachis**—the axis of a spike.
98. **Receptacle**—the axis of a flower stalk bearing the floral parts.
99. **Reniform**—kidney-shaped.
100. **Reticulate**—as in a network of veins in a leaf.
101. **Rhizome**—an underground stem, usually horizontal, from which shoots and roots may develop.
102. **Rosette**—a cluster of leaves crowded on very short internodes.
103. **Rugose**—wrinkled.
104. **Sagittate**—arrow-shaped.
*105. **Samara**—a dry, indehiscent fruit having a wing, e.g., maple.
*106. **Scape**—a leafless flower stem arising from the soil.
107. **Schizocarp**—a dry, dehiscent fruit in which the carpels separate at maturation.
108. **Sepal**—a single member of the calyx.
109. **Septum**—a partition within an organ.
*110. **Serrate**—with sharp teeth and directed forward.

111. **Sessile**—without a
112. **Silique**—a dry, deh a septum.
113. **Sori**—spore masses
*114. **Spadix**—a spike w by a spathe.
*115. **Spathe**—a large br
116. **Spatulate**—spade-s
*117. **Spike**—an inflores sessile to the pedu
118. **Stamen**—the male
119. **Standard** (in a pap
120. **Stigma**—the recep
121. **Stipule**—an appe species.
122. **Stolon**—a prostra a runner.
123. **Style**—that part ovary.
124. **Succulent**—fleshy
125. **Terrestrial**—plan
126. **Tomentose**—dens
127. **Tuber**—undergro the potato.
*128. **Umbel**—an indet originate at abou about the same l
*129. **Undulate**—a wa
130. **Variety**—a subd
131. **Whorled**—leaves
132. **Wings**—(in a pa
133. **Xerophyte**—a pl

Glossary

see illustration

*1. **Achene**—a dry, hard, indehiscent, single-seeded fruit with a single carpel.
2. **Acaulescent**—stemless
3. **Acuminate**—tapering to a point.
4. **Adnate**—united, grown together.
5. **Adventitious**—originating at other than the usual place; *roots* originating from any structure other than a root; *buds* arising from a part of the plant other than terminal or node.
6. **Alternate** (leaves)—one leaf at each node but alternating in direction.
7. **Annual**—a plant with a one-year life cycle.
8. **Anther**—that part of the stamen containing the pollen.
9. **Apetalous**—lacking petals.
10. **Apical**—terminal or summit.
11. **Axil**—the angle between a leaf and stem.
*12. **Berry**—a simple, fleshy fruit developed from a single ovule (loosely, any pulpy or juicy fruit).
13. **Biennial**—a plant with a two-year life cycle.
14. **Blade**—the expanded part of a leaf or leaflet.
*15. **Blossom**—the flower of a seed plant.
16. **Bract**—a specialized, modified leaf; of leaf-like structure.
17. **Bud**—a compressed stem; an underdeveloped stem.
18. **Bulb**—underground storage and reproductive organ with fleshy leaves called bulb scales.
19. **Calyx**—the outermost of the floral parts, composed of sepals.

*20. **Campanulate**—bell-shaped.
21. **Capitate**—shaped like a head.
*22. **Capsule**—a dry, dehiscent, multi-seeded fruit of more than one carpel.
23. **Carpel**—a leaf-like structure bearing ovules along the margins; a simple pistil.
*24. **Cauline**—related to an obvious stem or axis.
25. **Comose**—having tufts of hair.
*26. **Cordate**—heart-shaped.
27. **Corm**—an enlarged, underground stem, serving as a storage organ for food reserves.
28. **Corolla**—an inner cycle of floral organs, comprising the petals.
29. **Corymb**—a flat-topped, indeterminate flower cluster, with pedicels originating along a central peduncle; outer flowers open first.
30. **Cotyledons**—the first (seed) leaves of the embryo.
31. **Crenate**—toothed with rounded teeth.
32. **Crispate**—curled.
33. **Culm**—the stem of a grass or sedge.
34. **Cultivar**—a variety developed from known hybridization or origin.
35. **Cuneate**—triangular, wedge-shaped.
36. **Cyme**—a determinate flower cluster in which the central flower opens first.
37. **Deciduous**—plants that drop their leaves at the end of each season.
38. **Dehiscent**—opening of an anther or a fruit, permitting escape of pollen or seeds.
39. **Dentate**—toothed along the margins, apex sharp.
40. **Dichotomous**—divided into pairs; forked branches roughly equal.
41. **Dicotyledonous**—having two cotyledons.

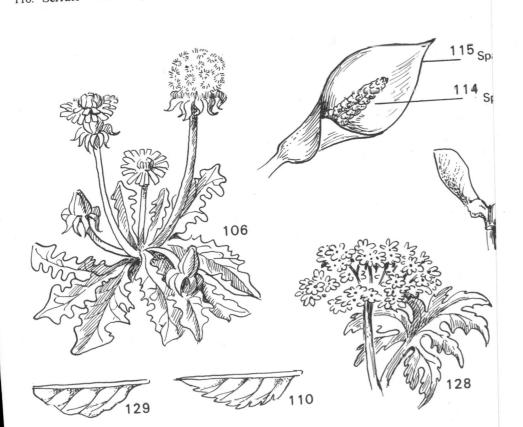

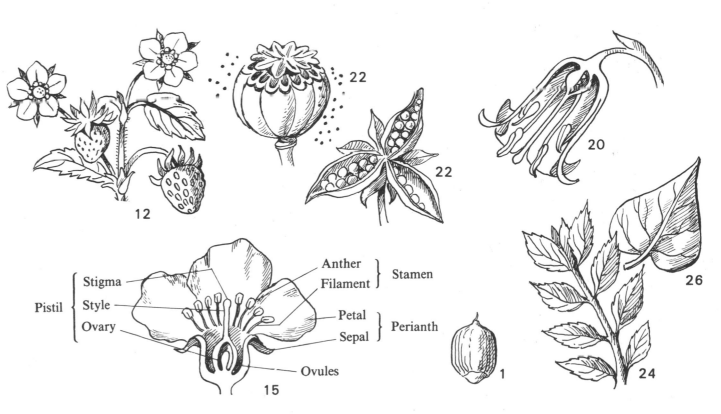

42. **Digitate** (leaves)—with leaflets arising from the apex of the petiole.
43. **Dioecious**—a species having male and female flowers on different, individual plants.
44. **Distichous**—in two vertical ranks, as the leaves of grasses.
*45. **Drupe**—a simple fleshy fruit, single carpel, with a hard endocarp containing the seed, e.g., the peach.
46. **Embryo**—a rudimentary plant.
47. **Entire**—without dentation or division.
48. **Epiphyte**—a plant that grows on another but is not parasitic.
49. **Fasciated**—an abnormally wide and flat stem.
50. **Filament**—the part of the stamen supporting the anther.
51. **Follicle**—a dry, dehiscent fruit with a single carpel, which dehisces along the ventral suture.
52. **Frond**—the leaf of a fern.
53. **Glabrous**—without hairs or pubescence.
54. **Glaucous**—covered with a whitish "bloom."
55. **Habit**—the general appearance of a plant.
*56. **Head**—a short, dense inflorescence, frequently with ray flowers around the margins and *tubular* disk flowers inside.
57. **Herbaceous**—non-woody.
58. **Hirsute**—hairy.
59. **Humus**—incompletely decomposed organic materials in the soil.
60. **Hybrid**—the result of a cross between two parents differing in genetic composition.
61. **Hydrophyte**—water loving; a plant adapted to wet conditions; capable of growing in water.
62. **Imbricate**—overlapping vertically or spirally.
63. **Indehiscent**—fruits remaining closed at maturity.
64. **Inflorescence**—the arrangement of flowers in a cluster; a complete flower cluster.
65. **Internode**—the part of a stem between two nodes.

6⊆. ⸺cre—a ⸺florescence.
67. **Keel**—the tw⸺ers, e.g., pea.
*68. **Lanceolate**—⸺widening abo⸺
*69. **Legume**—dry⸺along both s⸺
70. **Lenticils**—sⵊ⸺
71. **Lenticular**—⸺
72. **Ligulate**—st⸺
73. **Ligule**—a th⸺grasses.
74. **Lip**—one p⸺different siz⸺
75. **Monoecious**⸺plant.
76. **Morpholog**⸺
77. **Needle**—th⸺as pine and⸺
78. **Node**—poi⸺
*79. **Opposite** (⸺other.
*80. **Palmate**—⸺
*81. **Panicle**—a⸺
*82. **Papilionac**⸺ard keel a⸺
83. **Pedicel**—t⸺
84. **Peduncle**—⸺
85. **Perrenial**—⸺die after f⸺
86. **Perfect** (f⸺same flow⸺

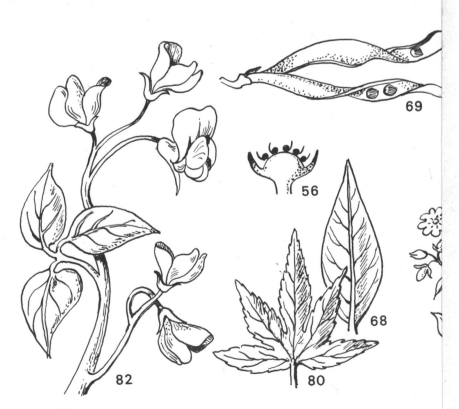

69

56

82 80 68

Index of plants mentioned

Abies cephalonica 18
Abies concolor 18
Abies Nordmanniana 18
Abies Pinsapo 18
Acacia 42
Acacia Baileyana 42
Acacia cultriformis 42
Acacia decurrens 42
Acacia Farnesiana 42
Acacia Julibrissin 42
Acacia longifolia 42
Acacia podalyiaeolia 42
Acacia retinodes 42
Acacia spectabilis 42
Acer japonicum 47
Acer Negundo 45
Acer palmatum 8, 46, 47
Acer platanoides 45
Acer polymorphum 46
Acer Pseudo-Platanus 44, 45
Aesculus carnea 47
Aesculus Hippocastanum 47
Aesculus Pavia 47
Albizzia 42
Albizzia Julibrissin 42
Araucaria araucana 28
Araucaria excelsa 28
Araucaria imbricata 28
Ash 44
Aucuba japonica 60
Azaleas 55
Barberry 7
Beech 34, 35
Berberis buxifolia 7
Berberis Thunbergii 7
Betula alba 32
Betula pendula 32
Betula pubescens 32
Betula papyrifera 32
Birch 32
Box 61
Box-elder 45
Broadleaves 29
Broom 54
Buckeye 47
Buckthorn 6, 7
Buddleia 6
Bush honeysuckle 12
Butterfly bush 6
Buxus balearica 61
Buxus sempervirens 61
Calycanthus praecox 50
Campsis radicans 53
Carpinus Betulus 33
Carpinus caroliniana 33
Catalpa bignonioides 49
Ceanothus 6, 7
Cedar 21
Cedrus atlantica 21
Cedrus Deodara 21
Cedrus libana 21
Celtis australis 37
Celtis occidentalis 37
Cephalotaxus Fortunei 27
Cercis canadensis 43
Cercis chinensis 43
Cercis Siliquastrum 43
Chaenomeles japonica 6, 7, 8
Chaenomales lagenaria 56
Chamaecyparis 7, 26
Chamaecyparis Lawsoniana 26

Chamaecyparis nootkatensis 26
Chamaecyparis obtusa 26, 27
Chamaecyparis pisifera 26, 27
Cherry laurel 59
Christ's thorn 7
Chimonanthus praecox 6, 50
Citrus trifoliata 7
Cornus 6, 9
Cornus florida 6
Cotoneaster 6, 7, 64
Cotoneaster adpressa 64
Cotoneaster bullata 64
Cotoneaster Dammeri 64
Cotoneaster Dielsiana 64
Cotoneaster horizontalis 64
Cotoneaster integerrima 64
Cotoneaster salicifolia 64
Cotoneaster tomentosa 64
Crataegus 6
Crataegus Oxyacantha 63
Cryptomeria japonica 24
Cupressus arizonica 25
Cupressus macrocarpa 25, 26
Cupressus sempervirens 25
Cypress 25, 26
Cytisus 7, 54
Cytisus Laburnum 54
Cytisus purpureus 54
Cytisus scoparius 54
Cytisus sessilifolius 54
Daphne 7
Deutzia 6, 8, 9, 12
Diervilla 12
Dogwood 6, 9
Douglas fir 19
Elaeagnus pungens 7
Erica carnea 6, 7
Euonymus japonicus 60, 61
Fagus sylvatica 34, 35
Fir 18, 19
Firethorn 6, 7, 63
Forsythia 9, 56
Forsythia intermedia 56
Forsythia suspensa 56
Forsythia viridissima 56
Fraxinus excelsior 44
Ginkgo 17
Ginkgo biloba 6, 17
Golden-Chain Tree 54
Hackberry 37
Hamamelis mollis 6, 50
Hawthorn 6
Heath 6, 7
Helianthemum 7
Hibiscus 6
Holly 60
Horse chesnut 47
Hydrangea 51
Hydrangea Hortensia 51
Hydrangea macrophylla 51
Hydrangea paniculata 51
Hydrangea petiolaris 51
Hypericum calycinum 7, 8
Ilex Aquifolium 60
Ilex cornuta 60
Ilex crenata 60
Ilex opaca 60
Incense cedar 26
Italian cypress 25
Jasminum nudiflorum 12
Japanese pagoda tree 44, 45

Japanese quince 56
Japanese quince (dwarf) 6, 7, 8
Jasminum nudiflorum 12
Judas tree 43
Juglans nigra 29
Juniper 7
Juniperus 7
Kerria japonica 8
Laburnum 54
Laburnum anagyroides 54
Lagerstroemia 12
Libocedrus decurrens 26
Ligustrum ovalifolium 62
Ligustrum vulgare 62
Linden 48
Liquidambar Styraciflua 36
Liriodendron Tulipifera 39
Maclura aurantiaca 7
Magnolia 38, 39
Magnolia denudata 39
Magnolia grandiflora 38, 39
Magnolia liliflora 39
Magnolia purpurea 39
Magnolia Sieboldii 39
Magnolia Soulangeana 39
Magnolia stellata 39
Malus floribunda 41
Maple 45, 46, 47
Mimosa 42
Mock orange 6, 8, 9, 12
Monkey puzzle 28
Morus alba 44
Mulberry 44
Norfolk Island pine 28
Paliurus spina-Christi 7
Paulownia 9, 49
Paulownia Fortunei 49
Paulownia tomentosa 49
Philadelphus 6, 8, 9, 12
Picea Abies 7, 20
Picea Omorika 20
Picea orientalis 20
Picea pungens 20
Pine 22, 23
Pinus Cembra 23
Pinus Mugo var. Mughus 23
Pinus nepalensis 22, 23
Pinus nigra 23
Pinus Pinea 23
Pinus Strobus 22, 23
Pittosporum crassifolium 59
Pittosporum eriolama 59
Pittosporum tenuifolium 59
Pittosporum Tobira 59
Pittosporum undulatum 59
Pittosporum viridiflorum 59
Plane tree 35
Platanus acerifolia 35
Platanus occidentalis 35
Platanus orientalis 35
Plum 40
Poplar 31, 39
Populus nigra var. italica 31
Potentilla fruticosa 7
Privet 62
Prunus 40, 41, 59
Prunus avium 41
Prunus cerasifera 41
Prunus Cerasus 41
Prunus japonica 41
Prunus Laurocerasus 59

Prunus lusitanica 59
Prunus serrulata 40, 41
Prunus subhirtella 41
Prunus triloba 41
Pseudotsuga Douglasii 19
Pseudotsuga taxifolia 19
Pterocarya fraxinifolia 29
Pyracantha 6, 7
Pyracantha angustifolia 63
Pyracantha coccinea 63
Pyracantha crenato-serrata 63
Redbud 43
Rhododendron 55
Rhododendron catawbiense 55
Rhus 9
Rhus typhina 8
Rosa 52, 53
Rosa Wichuriana 53
Rose 52, 53
Salisburia adiantifolia 17
Salix 9
Salix alba 30, 31
Salix babylonica 30, 31
Salix blanda 30
Salix Caprea 31
Salix cinerea 31
Salix fragilis 30
Salix Matsundana 31
Salix purpurea 31
Salix sepulcralis 30
Sciadopitys verticillata 24
Sequoia sempervirens 23
Sequoiadendron giganteum 23
Silk tree 42
Sophora japonica 44, 45
Spiraea 9
Spruce 7, 20
Sumac 8, 9
Sweet gum 36
Sycamore 35
Tamarix 9
Tamarix africana 40
Tamarix gallica 40
Tamarix parviflora 40
Tamarix pentandra 40
Taxodium distichum 24
Taxus baccata 27
Tilia 48
Tilia americana 48
Tilia argentea 48
Tilia cordata 48
Tilia europaea 48
Tilia petiolaris 48
Tilia platyphyllos 48
Tilia tomentosa 48
Trumpet vine 53
Tulip tree 39
Viburnum 6, 57
Viburnum Carlesii 57
Viburnum Lantana 57
Viburnum Opulus 57
Viburnum rhytidophyllum 57
Viburnum Tinus 7, 57
Walnut 29
Willow 9, 30, 31
Wistaria floribunda 53
Wistaria frutescens 53
Wistaria sinensis 53
Yew 27

The conifers

Ginkgo

Ginkgo biloba (or Maidenhair tree) is sometimes listed in horticultural encyclopedias under the name *Salisburia adiantifolia* (family Ginkgoaceae). Although it is not a conifer, it has some similarities with such trees and for practical purposes is discussed with them.

The name of the genus is Chinese and signifies "trees with silver fruits". The two-lobed leaves give it its species name. Kaempfer discovered it in 1690 and published a description in 1712; in about 1730 the plant was grown for the first time in Europe in the Botanical Garden in Utrecht, and was introduced to Britain about 1750.

Morphology. It is a tall tree (60 to 120 feet), with a thick, erect trunk, few branches, a pyramidal top when young, later broadening, irregular, and always rather bare. The leaves are deciduous, fan-shaped with a notch at the tip, on a long pedicel, membranous and veined, light green, attached in groups of 3 to 5 to the short lateral branches set sparsely on the limbs. The bark is greyish, cracked, with rounded crests.

The male and female flowers are on separate plants; the male flowers are catkins and in clusters; the female are paired at the tip of a long peduncle (usually one of these aborts). The fruit is a drupe, fleshy, yellowish, and ill-smelling when ripe, whose ovoid seed has a thin shell.

Origin. This plant, botanically isolated from the monocots and dicots of the plant world, must be considered a living fossil, the sole representative of a group of plants that had their peak perhaps 200 million years ago.

Varieties. The varieties of the ginkgo are the following: *aurea*, with yellow leaves during the summer; *fastigiata*, with pyramidal habit; *laciniata*, with deeply-incised leaves; *pendula*, with weeping branches; *variegata*, with variegated-yellow leaves.

Cultivation. It is a hardy species, resistant to cold, liking deep, cool soil. It does not grow rapidly, but puts out long shoots at an early age.

This handsome tree can be planted in isolation or as a shade tree for streets in the south, or against south or west walls elsewhere. Plant only male trees to avoid the odour of the fruit. It is particularly picturesque in spring, when it puts out its beautiful, light-green leaves, and above all in autumn, when the top acquires a vivid golden colour. The wood has no use. The kernel of the seed, having a sweetish taste and being slightly resinous, is edible.

It is reproduced by seed (fertile only if trees of the two sexes are near each other), by cuttings, and by grafting. It is especially resistant to insects and diseases, and to air-pollutants, making it a good street tree in the south.

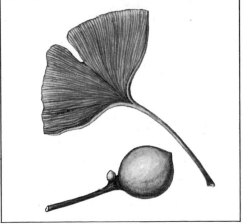

1. Specimen of *Ginkgo biloba* in autumnal colour.

2. Leaf and fruit.

3. Branch with the characteristic fan-shaped foliage.

4

5

6

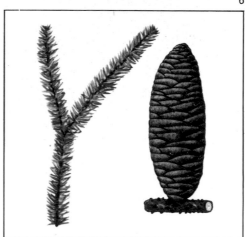

7

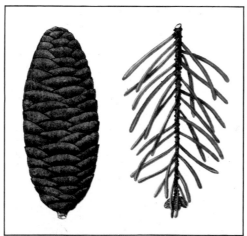

8

9

Spanish fir

Abies Pinsapo, family Pinaceae
The name of this species derives from the Spanish dialect term for this tree.

Origin. It was introduced into European culture in 1838 by the botanist Boissier and met the immediate approval of landscape architects. In Britain specimens had been cultivated since the early seventeenth century.

Morphology. This is a tree of great height, which can surpass 75 feet, with a sturdy trunk, having many nodes and covered with dark grey bark, smooth on young trees, fissured on older specimens.

The top is pyramidal, rather broad, not very regular, with horizontal branches. The needles are short, thick, rigid, not very sharp, dark green, and the needles are set rather thickly all around the branch and more or less perpendicular to it.

The cones, lacking a peduncle, are erect, as in all the firs, and are brown or purple-brown, formed of numerous almost triangular scales, very broad and close together. The cone is persistent after seeds are shed.

Varieties. The principal horticultural species are the varieties: *aurea*, shrubby, with silver-grey needles; *glauca*, with glaucous needles; *hamondii*, dwarf, with a short trunk, broad branches spread out on the ground, and small needles.

Cultivation. This pine is an endemic species of the extreme southern tip of Spain. It lives in sparse forests, at altitudes of 3,500 to 6,000 feet, in areas heavily affected by grazing and by fires that hinder the renovation of flora. It is particularly adapted to a Mediterranean climate, and is tolerant to drought and low humidity; it is not tolerant to cold and is injured by temperatures below 5 degrees. It has no particular preference in soils, but does well on sandy loam.

The Spanish pine is a species of slow growth that has limited forest use. It is grown primarily as an ornamental tree.

Propagation is by seed, which is difficult to preserve and has a low level of germination. Seed is covered lightly in sowing; the shade-loving seedlings should be carefully protected from the sun and be kept moist. They may be propagated in the greenhouse by grafting, a terminal shoot being used as the scion; or a side shoot may be used as long as it is erect in growth.

Other species. Other species of fir are often grown in European parks. The Greek fir (*A. cephalonica*) has pungent foliage; it is a hardy species, resistant to summer drought, prefers full sun, suited to calcareous soil; it cannot stand a hard freeze. The Caucasian fir (A. *Nordmanniana*) has blunt needles, shiny on top, covering the branches thickly.

A. concolor, white fire, is native to the south-western United States, has long, sparse needles, silver-grey on both sides. *A. balsamea* is a favourite species for Christmas trees (Balsam fir), and *A. lasiocarpa* is the Rocky Mountain Fir.

10

11

13

14

15

Douglas fir

Pseudotsuga taxifolia or *P. Douglasii*, family Pinaccac

The term *Pseudotsuga* means "false Tsuga" because of the resemblance of their needles to those of hemlock; *taxifolia* means "with foliage like yew".

Origin This magnificent tree was discovered by Archibald Menzies on Vancouver Island in 1795 and introduced by David Douglas to Great Britain in about 1826.

Morphology. The Douglas fir reaches 200 to 300 feet, placing it among the taller trees. When young, its bark is grey and smooth, dotted, however, with small blisters full of resin resembling cedar in aroma; later the bark splits, becoming corky, and one may observe two kinds of secondary bark, one of plates and another with deep longitudinal, sparse cracks.

The habit of isolated trees is pyramidal, with a long, regular, pointed top; the branches are in somewhat regular whorls, the upper ones horizontal, the lower ones bending downwards.

The needles are attached to the branches at right angles, like teeth of a comb; they are linear, flat, soft, green, marked on the lower side with two blue-green lines of stomata.

The cones are easily differentiated from those of other conifers; they are ovoid, reddish brown, with woody scales that are thin, rounded or convex, alternate, with longer trilobed bracts, and with a sharply pointed central lobe.

Varieties. Species thriving in the wild in western portions of North America, from British Columbia to Mexico, include: var. *menziesii*, (green or Oregon Douglas fir); var. *glauca* with smaller leaves and cones; and var. *caesia*, leaves bluish green and intermediate between the two preceding in morphology and ecology.

The variety *glauca*, commonly known as the blue or Colorado Douglas fir, is a handsome ornamental tree, not as tall, with intensely blue-green foliage and similar bracts of cones, turned up, however, when ripe, and a longer central lobe; this variety is more resistant to dry climates and to frost than is the green Douglas fir.

Other horticultural varieties include *fastigiata*, *pendula*, *brevibracteata*, *argentea* (with silver-white leaves), *aurea* (leaves at first light yellow), and *Fretsii* (leaves short and broad).

Cultivation. In general the green Douglas fir needs acid, deep, fertile, and well-drained soil and a humid, maritime climate; its resistance to frost and late cold spells is related to the production of seed. When young, it grows best in light shade; later it becomes sun-loving. It may suffer from strong winds, but thrives on abundant rainfall.

The wood is valued for many uses, including building, railway sleepers, and masts; its warm, reddish colour and regular, fine veining are prized for plywood.

This long-lived and fast-growing plant is re-produced by seed sown 1 inch deep in open beds during March, and transplanting the seedlings when two years old. The horticultural varieties are propagated by grafting.

One of the most common diseases to afflict this tree is caused by a fungus, *Phomopsis pseudotsugae* which causes several types of damage. The leading and lateral shoots die back to about 12 inches, with leaves going brown and yellow and quickly falling off. Cuts on the bark may be affected and this in time leads to girdling. Another fairly common ailment is known as resin bleeding. At the base of the branches and on lesions in the main trunk there is a profuse resin exudation. This condition is probably caused by several types of fungi.

---

4. *Abies cephalonica.*

5, 8. *Abies concolour* and detail.

6. *Abies Nordmanniana* and its cone.

7, 9. Details of *Abies Pinsapo.*

10, 11. Branches with young cones of *Pseudotsuga taxifolia* var. *glauca* and var. *viridis.*

12. *Pseudotsuga taxifolia* and its cone.

13. Female flower of the same plant.

14. View of the trunk of an old specimen of *P. taxifolia.*

15. Branch of the same species.

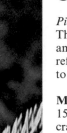

16

19

Colorado spruce

Picea pungens, family Pinaceae
The name of this genus was already in use among the Romans, who derived it from *pix*, referring to the pitch; the ending *pungens* is due to the aromatic foliage.

Morphology. This is a tree that may reach 150 feet; it has a brownish-grey bark deeply cracked and scaly in old specimens; the top is narrowly pyramidal, quite regular in shape if grown in the open.

The needles are solitary, linear, rigid, incurved, sharp and blue-green, attached all around the twig, which is light orange-brown.

The cones are pendulous, cylindrical, light brown and shiny at maturity, with soft scales that are blunt at the top, toothed and wavy.

Varieties. The variety most cultivated, for its silvery blue-green foliage, is the *Kosteriana*, with pendulous branches; there are also the varieties *argentea*, *viridis*, *aurea*, *flavescens*, *prostrata*, and *tabuliformis*.

Cultivation. It is a plant of high altitudes in the Rocky Mountains, from Montana to New Mexico, where it grows at 5,500 to 10,000 feet. It is a hardy species, resistant to cold and to drought; it grows best where summers are cool and winters severe. It prefers full sun and tolerates wind and the polluted air of cities. The bluish forms are more delicate and can lose their original colour or even their needles from aphid infestation when planted in a mild climate. This spruce grows rather slowly and is long-lived.

This tree is frequently used ornamentally in gardens; if specimens with a more specialized appearance are desired, *Kosteriana* will make handsome spots of colour. Propagation in nature is by seed; cultivars are propagated by grafting.

Other species. Some other species of the genus *Picea* are cultivated as ornamentals, including the Common or Norway spruce (*Picea Abies*), the traditional Christmas tree. A forest plant of mountains and foothills, resistant to extremes of weather, this tree is suited to planting in any soil, provided that the winters are cold and summers not too dry. Because of its shallow root system it may be uprooted by strong winds. It will not tolerate heavy air pollution. At low altitudes, young specimens are often attacked by an aphid. Its timber is known as white deal.

A dwarf form of the Common spruce is *P. Ellwangeriana*, and a weeping variety is *P. pendula*. *P. Gregoryana*, a very dwarf form and conical, grows to 2 feet.

The Serbian spruce is similar (*Picea Omorika*). The Oriental spruce is rather elegant (*P. orientalis*), and is found throughout Turkey and the Caucasus. It has a regular, pyramidal top, its dense branching down to the ground, and its short-needled foliage. The cones are small.

17

18

20

21

16, 17, 19. *Picea pungens* and its twigs.

18. *Picea pungens* var. *Kosteriana*.

20. *Picea Abies*.

21. *Picea Abies* var. *pendula*.

Atlas cedar

Cedrus atlantica, family Pinaceae
The name of the genus derives from the Greek *kedros*; the species name indicates its origin, the Atlas chain of mountains in Morocco.

Morphology. The trunk is thick and strong; the branches, frequently ascending; the top, broad, but sparse; the habit, pyramidal with an erect terminal shoot when young, in old specimens assuming flat layers. It can attain a height of 100 to 125 feet. The needles are short, stiff, sharp, and rectangular; they are sparse on new growth and attached in spirals on small lateral branches.

The cones are rather large, erect, bottle-shaped, resinous with membranous scales that are short and wide, closely shingled, of a violet purple colour before ripening. The bark is grey and smooth in young specimens, but later develops into brown scales.

Varieties. The variety most known and widespread is *glauca* with blue-grey needles. *Argenta* has grey-blue foliage, and *aurea* golden foliage.

Origin. It is native to the Atlas mountains of Morocco and some Algerian mountains at 5,500 to 7,000 feet, in humid to semi-dry climates.

Cultivation. It requires a well-drained soil and ample space, preferring full sun. It tolerates dry summers and severe cold as low as 25°C (−10°F).

It is an important plant in its country of origin and is used for reforestation in sub-Mediterranea zones. It does particularly well in seaside areas. In gardens it is employed in isolated groups on expanses of lawn; to form a handsome colour contrast, the variety *glauca* may be used. It is propagated by seed, by cuttings, or by grafting. The fall of needles in winter in urban areas is blamed on smog.

Other species. *Cedrus Deodara*, the Deodar cedar has longer needles of a slightly bluish green and a curved top. The oldest cedar in England at Brethby Park, Derbyshire, planted in 1676, is a Cedar of Lebanon, *C. libani*; in old specimens this has a decidedly flattened top.

22. *Cedrus atlantica.*

23, 24. *Cedrus atlantica* var *glauca*, and detail.

25. *Cedrus Deodara.*

26. *Cedrus libani* (Cedar of Lebanon).

27

28

Pine

Genus *Pinus*, family Pinaceae
The major description here is of *Pinus nepalensis*, the Himalaya white pine, otherwise known as *Pinus griffithii*.

Morphology. *P. nepalensis* is a pine with elegant habit, characterized by great height (100 feet in cultivation, 170 in nature), a rather rigid top, shaped in a pyramid, with branches more or less horizontal, arching a little upwards at the ends, regularly whorled and with abundant needles that are long and thin, bluish-green, soft, pendant, and clustered in groups of five.

The cones are about 10 inches long, cylindrical, attenuated at both ends, resinous, formed of oval scales with a thick spatulate tip that opens wide at maturity. The timber reaches maturity at about 80 years.

Varieties. There are two varieties, not often cultivated, *monophylla*, with isolated needles, and *zebrina*, with needles striped green and yellow. Hybrid forms of this plant with *P. Strobus* are known in cultivation, characterized by shorter and not so weeping needles, as are hybrids with *P. Ayacahuite*. The latter have less resistance to cold, being native to Mexico. These hybrids are usually the result of planting seeds gathered from trees in parks where cross-fertilization is enhanced.

Origin. The *P. nepalensis* is a native of the Himalayan forests from 5,500 and 13,000 feet up, and from Afghanistan to Nepal.

Cultivation. In culture it behaves as in the wild—resistant to cold, adapted to gravelly or sandy soils. It prefers a humid climate and is somewhat resistant to air pollutants; it grows rapidly but has a short life in cultivation.

It is frequently used in parks and gardens and occasionally as a street tree.

In timber-producing countries *P. nepalensis* is often planted for its soft, light wood, which is used for woodworking and paper pulp.

This tree is more resistant to blister rust and air pollution than other white pines.

Other species. Many other pines are grown as ornamentals: the white pine (*Pinus Strobus*) is a close relative of *P. nepalensis*, and is a native of North America, from the Great Lakes to the Appalachians. It is distinguished by shorter needles, in erect brushes, and cones smaller (about 4 inches) although otherwise similar. It is an excellent ornamental that becomes most attractive later than *P. nepalensis* because its rapid growth and shorter needles leave a sparse top when young. It is also planted in countries with good summer rainfall and cold winters, to produce lumber for woodworking and for paper pulp. The tree is attacked by blister rust, which causes cankers and the death of the plant.

In hillside gardens the Swiss Stone Pine (*P. Cembra*) makes a good effect. The species is slow-growing, and has clusters of five needles. In the Mediterranean region, the Italian Stone Pine, *P. Pinea*, is a principal element of the landscape, with its characteristic umbrella-shaped top and paired needles.

The pine often used in more difficult situations

29

30

31

32

33

34

(heavy, dry, calcareous soil) is the Austrian pine (*P. nigra*), which exists in several forms and is a good shelter tree.

For rock gardens and for sustaining terraces is the dwarf Mugo pine (*P. Mugo* var. *Mughus*), with prostrate, globose form, of Central European origin. A dwarf form suitable for rockeries is *P. Watereri*.

---

27. *Pinus nepalensis*, Himalaya White Pine.

28. *Pinus Strobus*, white pine.

29. *Pinus Pinea*, Italian Stone Pine.

30. *Pinus nigra*, Austrian Pine.

31. *Pinus Mugo* var. *Mughus*, dwarf Mugo pine.

Giant sequoia

Sequoiadendron giganteum, family Taxodiaceae. The name of the genus means tree (from the Greek *dendron*) of Sequoia, a Cherokee Indian of the United States of the eighteenth century who invented the Cherokee alphabet.

This splendid tree was discovered by David Douglas in 1831 and introduced into Great Britain by Lobb in 1854. Douglas, a famous plant hunter, was gored to death by a bull while on an expedition.

Morphology. The sequoia is the giant of plants, reaching 300 feet or more in the natural state, with an enormous circumference (e.g. 100 feet, in the specimen called General Sherman).

The species has exceptional longevity (perhaps beyond 3,000 years), which puts it in second place among the most ancient living beings (the first is held by specimens of Bristle-Cone Pine *Pinus aristata* of the Rocky Mountains, more than 4,600 years old).

The trunk is massive, narrowly pyramidal, enlarged at the base, characterized by a very thick, fibrous, spongy base with deep and longitudinal cracks. The top is dense, typically conical, and close-packed, formed of branches bending towards the lower parts.

The needles are small, alternate, scale-shaped, imbricate (edged like tiles), covering the twigs.

The cone is ovoid, formed of wedge-shaped scales with a furrowed, rhomboid tip.

The tree is susceptible to the fungus *Botrytis cinerea*, or grey mould.

Varieties. Some varieties are known: *aureum, glaucum,* and *pendulum.*

Origin. The giant sequoia originates from a limited area of California (the Sierra Nevadas) at from 5,000 to 8,000 feet, in a temperate climate with abundant snowfall.

Cultivation. In culture this tree needs deep loam and prefers areas with damp climate and air. It tolerates winter cold and shade quite well. Because of the dimensions it reaches, it is suited to planting as a single specimen in large parks and for forming majestic lanes.

It is reproduced by seed, by cuttings, or by grafting; it re-sprouts easily from stumps which is rare among conifers.

Other species. *Sequoia sempervirens*, the Redwood, also cultivated, is a tree that can attain similar heights, although smaller in diameter. It has flat, almost comb-like needles about one inch long and mostly in two ranks.

It originates from the costal areas of northern California and needs high summer humidity and winters that are not too severe. It grows rapidly, and it is long-lived. It was introduced into Britain in the mid-nineteenth century.

---

32. Trunk of *Sequoiadendron giganteum*.

33, 34. *Sequoia sempervirens* and detail.

35

38

36

39

37

40

Bald cypress

Taxodium distichum, family Taxodiaceae
The name of the genus refers to a similarity of the needles of those of the yew (*Taxus*); *distichum* means "in a double row", referring to the arrangement of the needles on the twigs. It is sometimes known as the swamp cypress.

Morphology. It is a large tree with deciduous foliage (an exception among conifers), 100 to 135 feet tall, with a top somewhat irregular when old. The trunk is straight, thick at the base, and it has a rather thin bark, which is reddish-brown, fibrous, and scaly. In swampy soil with poor soil aeration the peculiar cypress knees grow vertically from the roots; their purpose is to bring air to the roots when the soil is covered with water.

The needles are linear, herbaceous, light green, whitish underneath, set like the teeth of a comb in the sides of the twigs, which drop with them in the autumn.

The cones are almost spherical, reddish, woody or cork-like, rough, and terminate in a hard, short point.

The variety *pendens* has drooping branches.

Origin. The bald cypress is native to the coasts and rivers of the southern United States, where it grows in flooded or swampy zones, although in cultivation it adapts well to dry soil.

Cultivation. Although it comes from a temperate or warm-temperate climate, it is resistant to cold, except for young plants. In Britain the bald cypress does well on lawns in a sheltered position where there is plenty of sun. It is used in parks, especially near water, where it makes its greatest growth, and so does well in soil with poor drainage. Its foliage is very colourful in autumn, becoming a rusty red. Propagation is by seed or cuttings.

Other species. To the same family belongs another decorative conifer, *Cryptomeria japonica*, native to Japan and China, evergreen, with awl-shaped needles and a serated and conical top; in old specimens the straight trunk has a handsome reddish-brown bark that sheds. It is recommended for cool but not too cold climates. The variety *elegans* is especially appreciated for its fine foliage and its rusty-red colour in winter. It is low growing. Besides propagation by seed, *Cryptomeria* may be propagated by cuttings or air layering.

Another tree of this family, the Umbrella Pine (*Sciadopitys verticillata*), is evergreen, usually 50 to 60 feet tall, and has a rather thin top. Some of the leaves are scaly and some are long, arranged in whorls. Cultural requirements are similar to cryptomeria but this slow-growing tree is more resistant to cold, even so it should be sheltered from piercing winds.

35, 36. *Taxodium distichum* and detail of its trunk and branches.

37. Twig with cones of *Taxodium distichum*.

38. *Cryptomeria japonica*.

39, 40. *Sciadopitys verticillata* and detail.

41

Italian cypress

Cupressus sempervirens var. *stricta*, family Cupressaceae

The early Romans used this plant and gave it its name "*sempervirens*", meaning evergreen. It has been cultivated since ancient times and has featured in much romantic poetry and prose typified by Lord Byron who wrote in *The Bride of Abydos*:

Know ye the land where the cypress and myrtle
Are emblems of deeds that are done in their clime;
Where the rage of the vulture, the love of the turtle,
Now melt into sorrow, now madden to crime?

To the Romans the Italian cypress was a tree of death, probably for two reasons. As the tree grows old its foliage blackens, and once it is cut down it rarely grows again. The tree is often grown in cemeteries, even in Britain although the climate here is not suited to it.

In the past it was used for boat building—Alexander the Great used it to build his fleet.

Morphology. In the description of this tree, the var. *stricta*, commonly used as an ornamental, is referred to first, and then follows the diverse characteristics of another variety *horizontalis*. The Italian cypress is a tall tree (up to 100 feet), with a trunk which is not always circular in cross-section but exhibits, especially at the base, buttresses and ribbing, and is covered with a bark finely but not deeply cracked longitudinally, grey-brown, and fibrous. The top is typically compact, columnar or spindle-shaped, formed of abundant, erect branches with twigs completely covered by minute, scale-like, oval-obtuse needles, which are close together and dark green. The cones are spherical with woody scales.

Varieties. *C. sempervirens* var. *horizontalis*, has horizontal branches; the top is less dense and the tree has a pyramidal habit. It is sometimes used as the first step in reforestation and does well in groups as a windbreak.

Origin. Although widespread, the cypress exists today only under cultivation; it is believed to have originated in the eastern basin of the Mediterranean, from which it was distributed for ornamental use.

Cultivation. The cypress is a xerophile (tolerating drought) and quite a hardy tree, suited to poor, stony soils. It will not flourish in wet soil and prefers mild winters. Moderately shade loving, it is among the most long-lived trees; in Italy, specimens many centuries old are known.

This is the classic cypress of Tuscan and Umbrian districts of Italy. It is grown as an individual tree, and in southern Europe in rows for street plantings. It may be pruned to make hedges and screens. The wood resists insect damage and is used for furniture and in building.

Propagation is by seed; the young plants have difficulty becoming established if transplanted with bare roots, so seed is sown in containers and seedlings are transplanted with the ball of earth.

Other species. The Arizona cypress (*Cupressus arizonica*) is resistant to cold and has a tapering top. It is usually pruned so that it remains dense and full.

A species native to California is *C. macrocarpa*. Monterey Cypress, with a dense, broad top. Variety *lutea* has yellow leaves when young.

---

41. Group of Italian cypresses (*Cupressus sempervirens* var. *stricta*).

42. Detail of the top of the same species.

43. *Cupressus arizonica*. Arizona cypress.

44. *Cupressus macrocarpa*, Monterey cypress.

45

47

48

False-cypress

Chamaecyparis Lawsoniana, family Cupressaceae This plant (the name in Greek means "small cypress") is called Lawson's cypress. Despite its common name, the genus is only related to the true cypress. *Chamaecyparis nootkatensis* will hybridize with *Cupressus macrocarpa*, however.

Morphology. This tree is very tall in the wild (up to 160 feet); in cultivation it does not reach this height and is sometimes dwarf. The shape is conical, the head dense, the bark brown and deeply fissured longitudinally. The small, scale-like leaves completely cover the branchlets in four rows, the branchlets are opposite, giving the branches a frond-like appearance. The cone is small.

Varieties. The varieties are numerous and are distinguished by the foliage colouration, those with a columnar habit (some with pendant branches), those with a spreading habit, and the dwarfs.

Among the foliage variants are the following: *albospica* (compact top, branchlets creamy white at the top); *argentea* (foliage silvery); *aurea* (golden yellow); *glauca* (leaves steel-blue); *lutea* (young growth bright yellow).

Among the columnar varieties are *Allumii* (with blue-green needles), *erecta*, *Fletcheri* (with awl-shaped needles when young), *Pottersii* (with needles of mixed types), and *pyramidalis alba* (with branch tips white in spring). The variety *filiformis* is one of the weeping types.

Varieties with a spreading habit include:

gracilis, *lycopodioides*, and others. Among small, slow-growing varieties there are *nana*, a globose, bright-green shrub, and *nana* f. *glauca*.

Origin. The Lawson cypress is native to the western United States, along the Pacific coast (Oregon and California). Rainfall is high and the summers are dry, although the air is humid.

Cultivation. It grows on many types of soils if deep, fertile, and well-drained. It is not harmed by cold and will tolerate shade. It is frequently used in closely-spaced groups because of its slender habit; a collection of varieties produces a good effect. It may also be used for hedging and screens. The typical Lawson cypress is reproduced by seed and the varieties from cuttings.

Other species. Two other species are frequently planted: the Hinoki cypress, *C. obtusa*, often variety *nana*; and Sawara cypress, *C. pisifera*, with varieties *filifera* and *filifera aurea*. To the same family belongs the incense-cedar (*Libocedrus decurrens*), somewhat resembling the Lawson cypress, with needles hanging from the twigs.

---

45. *Chamaecyparis Lawsoniana*, variety *globosa*.

46. *C. Lawsoniana* variety *aurea*.

47. Group of *Chamaecyparis Lawsonia*.

48. Detail of the cultivar Golden King.

Yews

Taxus baccata, family Taxaceae

The name of the genus was in use among the Romans; *baccata* means "berry-producing". This species is the Common yew. Due to its sombre appearance it is often seen in cemeteries and churchyards, and many poets have used its association with death.

Morphology. It is an evergreen, 30–50 feet tall, generally with more than one trunk, irregular in form with numerous broad, ascending branches supporting a wide, dense, concave top. The bark is reddish-brown, thin, and scale-like.

The leaves, similar to pine needles, are linear, flattened, sickle-shaped, dark green, pointed, attached to the twigs like a comb.

The plant is dioecious. Fruit on the female specimens at the end of summer are berry-like, red, open at the end. The seed and the foliage are poisonous.

Varieties. The botanical varieties are numerous and include: *adpressa* (with short, oval-oblong needles and low habit), *aurea*, *compacta*, *erecta*, *glauca*, *horizontalis*, *nana*, *procumbens*, and *stricta*.

Origin. This species is native to Europe and Northern Asia, near the coasts, but its numbers have been reduced because of the value of the wood for cabinet making or because the foliage is poisonous to livestock.

Cultivation. It prefers deep, fertile soil, but will also thrive in fissured, rocky soil; it requires good drainage. It tolerates cold and has great longevity (more than 1,000 years).

Used as isolated specimens and for hedges, it is easy to shape by pruning and is a favourite tree for clipping for topiary work, and is one of the trees used in the famous maze at Hampton Court Palace. It may be planted under tall trees and in northern exposures.

The wood is durable with a very fine grain, and with polish takes on a brilliant surface, so is used in veneers, inlays, and cabinet work. Reproduction of the species is by seed; the varieties are propagated by layering or cuttings in the greenhouse during summer or by grafting in spring on potted rootstock. Cuttings grow slowly and often remain shrubby.

Other species. The plum-yew, *Cephalotaxus Fortunei*, resembles yew although belonging to another family, Cephalotaxaceae, and is a tall shrub with many, pendant branches. The needles have two glaucous lines underneath and are somewhat longer. The fruit is the size and shape of an olive and brownish when ripe. It originated in China and is grown as an ornamental. It has several varieties. The Japanese Yew, *T. cuspidata* grows to 50 feet.

---

49. *Chamaecyparis obtusa* var. *gracilis*.

50. *Chamaecyparis pisifera* var. *filifera*.

51. Twig of *Taxus baccata*, with fruit.

52. *Taxus baccata* var. *stricta*.

53. Detail of *Cephalotaxus Fortunei* twig.

49

50

51

52

53

Monkey puzzle

Araucaria araucana = A. imbricata, family Araucariaceae

The name of the genus and species is from its country of origin, southern Chile, where the native people were called Araucans; the name imbricata is from the scale-like structure of the needles.

The plant was discovered about 1780 and introduced into Europe by Archibald Menzies in 1795, although for many years it continued to be a rarity. Menzies sailed with Captain Vancouver on voyages that took them along the coast of Chile, and it was from here that the botanist collected seeds of the monkey puzzle tree. Some of the plants grown from this seed were presented to the Royal Botanic Gardens at Kew. The last one died nearly a century later in 1892.

Morphology. This tree may reach 130 feet; the columnar trunk is usually branched to the ground. In old trees a secondary bark with plate-lets is formed; the trunk, after losing its needles, remains for many years marked by their scars. The limbs are in whorls of 4 to 9, horizontal or inclined downwards in the lower part and some-what upturned at the top; they are completely covered with thick, leathery, oval or lanceolate, pointed needles, which remain alive for 10 to 15 years and still persist when they become dry.

The monkey puzzle tree has male and female plants. The fruit is large, spherical-ovoid, formed of numerous wedge-shaped, lanceolate scales with a long point, leathery and woody; they do not always contain fertile seeds. The seeds are large, shiny and edible.

Varieties. Although not widespread, some varieties of this plant exist: *platifolia* has rather broad needles; *striata*, with trunk and needles striped yellow; *aurea*, with golden yellow needles.

Cultivation. The monkey puzzle lives in a temperate climate with winter snow and abundant rainfall, usually in hardwood forests. It prefers a moist, well-drained, acid soil. It does not tolerate rapid drops in temperature and needs a high, dry, and sheltered position not exposed to industrial smoke.

In view of its peculiar habit, this tree is best used in a single specimen or in small groups. But it can be mixed with other trees in a sheltered position, particularly where winters are harsh, to prevent dehydration of the branches and the resultant destruction of the symmetry that is the principal charm of the plant.

The monkey puzzle has no commercial use in Britain but produces valued timber in Chile, where at one time it was used in shipbuilding.

Araucaria is propagated by seed or by cuttings, a terminal shoot being used. There are also a number of greenhouse species originating in Australasia.

Other species. Another hardy species is *Araucaria araucana* var. *aurea*, with golden-tinted foliage.

---

54. *Araucaria araucana*, monkey puzzle tree.

Broadleaved trees

Black walnut

Juglans nigra, family Juglandaceae
Juglans is the ancient Latin name for the walnut; *nigra* refers to the dark colour of the bark. It was first grown in Britain about 1585.

Morphology. This is a tall tree, reaching 100 to 150 feet. The trunk is blackish, fissured at an early age. The tree has a broad crown, and is oval or rounded in form. The leaves are large, alternate, deciduous, odd-pinnate with numerous oval-lanceolate pointed, toothed leaflets, hairy beneath along the vein.

The plants are monoecious, the male flowers are green catkins, the females are single or clustered, with a small corolla and two short styles. The fruit is globose and contains a furrowed nut in a fleshy, yellowish-green epicarp with a pebbled, downy surface.

The nut is rough and hard and contains a tasty kernel. It is rather difficult to remove from the shell and thin-shelled types are sought.

Varieties. This tree varies little, but some horticultural varieties are grown.

Origin. The black walnut is native to eastern U.S., from Massachusetts to Florida and Texas. It was introduced into Britain in the late sixteenth century.

Cultivation. It does not tolerate crowding and dense shade, and is usually planted as a single tree in town gardens; it prefers a deep soil that is fertile and moderately moist but well-drained. In good soil it grows more rapidly, and lives up to 250 years.

In parks it is used as a specimen tree or in lanes; it needs adequate space.

The wood is used for furniture, panelling and gun stocks. The heart wood is dark-brown; the sapwood is whitish.

Propagation is by planting the mature nuts in the autumn. Viability is short-lived since, being rich in oil, the nuts easily become rancid; they may be preserved during winter in cool sand and sown $1\frac{1}{2}$ to 2 inches deep the following spring. Light soil is preferred because the plant produces a long tap root in heavy soil making transplanting after one or two years usually quite difficult. The black walnut is rarely attacked by insects.

Other species. Another ornamental Juglandaceae is *Pterocarya fraxinifolia*, the Caucasian Wing-Nut, also with compound leaves, many leaflets, and a pendant inflorescence. *J. regia*, found from the Caucasus to the Himalayas, grows to 60 feet, and *J. cinera*, the Butter Nut, of similar height is native to North America.

---

55. Fruiting branches of *Juglans nigra.*

56. Branches of *Pterocarya fraxinifolia*, with inflorescence.

57

58

Weeping willow

Salix babylonica, family Salicaceae

Salix is the Latin word for willow. The species name suggests Babylonia as the place of origin of the tree, although in reality it is native to China and Manchuria, from which it was introduced into Europe about 1730.

Napoleon was an admirer of the tree and one was planted by his tomb at St Helena. This died and more were planted to replace it.

Morphology. The tree is of small stature, reaching 30 to 40 feet, with a very broad crown; the limbs are spreading and bear numerous slender branches of a purplish or olive-green colour, which are drooping, giving the tree its common name.

Leaves are alternate, deciduous, narrow-lanceolate to lanceolate, pointed, on a short petiole, with minutely toothed edges. They are smooth, often bluish-green underneath.

The plant is dioecious and the flowers appear in spring along with the foliage. The flowers are soft catkins; the males are yellow, the females green. Fruits have white, cottony hairs and are carried by the wind. Female trees of the willow outnumber the male.

Varieties. A very distinct variety is *crispa*, in which the leaves are twisted to form a ring. Variety *aurea* has golden branches. Also in cultivation are *S. sepulcralis* and *S. blanda*, hybrids of *S. babylonica* with *S. alba* and *S. fragilis*, respectively. Propagation is by cuttings of shoots or stems in moist soil in October.

59

Lombardy poplar

Cultivation. Weeping willow requires moist or at least cool soil. It is much used as an isolated specimen in gardens, mirrored in lakes or streams, but too often it is incongruously mixed with plants of different form. The wood, soft, light and brittle, has no practical value.

It propagates with ease from cuttings which need no particular care.

The major damage to willows comes from infestations by defoliating and boring insects. The tree is subject to breakage in high winds.

Other species. Other willows to use in moist, sandy soil that are ornamental in winter are the Purple Osier, *S. purpurea*, with branches of a brilliant purple colour, and *S. alba* var. *vitellina*, with yellow branches. *S. alba* var. *calva* is used for making cricket bats. *S. Caprea* supplies wood for scythe and rake handles, hoops, poles and crates.

S. Matsudana var. *tortuosa* is a relatively recent introduction from China, where it is called Lung Chao Liu, curious in having twisted branches and curled leaves. It is sometimes called corkscrew willow. *S. viminalis*, the Osier Willow, is grown for its branches used in the making of baskets. It grows from 10 to 20 feet.

---

57. *Salix babylonica*, weeping willow.

58. *Salix alba*, white willow.

59. Leaves of *Salix Caprea* (above left), *S. cinerea* (above right), and *S. alba*, with catkins.

Populus nigra var. *italica*, family *Saliacceae* Considered a variety of the black poplar, the term *italica* indicates its probable origin in Italy. *Populus* is a name given by the early Romans.

Morphology. This tree is well known for its slender, towering habit. The numerous branches from the base to the top of the trunk ascend almost vertically, as do the secondary branches, forming a compact, spindle-shaped top that moves with the wind. It can attain 100 to 130 feet.

The brown-grey bark is coarsely fissured and rough; the trunk is straight, often with basal buttressing; the twigs are slender, somewhat angular; the leaves are almost rhombic, with a wedge-shaped base and a pointed tip, toothed near the tip and smooth; the long, elastic petiole allows them to rustle in the slightest breeze.

The black poplar is a dioecious plant, but no female plants of Lombardy poplar exist. The pendulous male catkins, reddish in colour, appear in abundance before the leaves. Female plants found are probably hybrids between this tree and other poplars.

Since this tree must be propagated vegetatively, we are dealing with a clone, probably derived from a bud mutation and then propagated for its aesthetic value. There have been indications of its cultivation since the beginning of the eighteenth century in Lombardy, where it probably originated: now it is known throughout the world. It is extremely fast growing, outstripping other trees in the garden, its annual growth being from three to five feet.

Cultivation. As is generally true of all poplars, this tree likes light, loose soil in which it may broadly spread its vigorous root system. It is resistant to cold but, because of the earliness of leafing-out in spring and the retaining of foliage late in autumn, it may be damaged by late-spring and early-autumn frosts. It has no special water requirements.

The Lombardy poplar is planted in rows along the sides of roads, lanes and waterways; it is also useful as a screen or a high fence.

The list of misfortunes that can strike poplars is very long; it may be that, after fruit trees, poplars are the broadleaved trees most attacked by disease and insects.

The Lombardy poplar is no exception, and may be infested by chewing and sucking insects, and by borers. Control is difficult. It is susceptible to rust and other diseases. Several fungi attack the wood, and in damp places *Armillaria* may develop on the roots. Bacteriosis, rather dangerous on some poplars, does not infest the Lombardy. The tree is also susceptible to frost damage, and to breakage in high winds.

Other species. *P. alba*, sometimes called Abele or White Poplar is an ornamental species common in Britain, Europe and northern Asia. Its leaves are green above and white beneath. Its variety *Richardii* has leaves yellow above, white beneath.

60, 61. *Populus nigra* var. *italica*. Lombardy poplar.

Birch

Betula pendula, family Betulaceae
The genus is an old Latin name; the species name refers to the drooping habit of the secondary branches. The common name is Silver birch. It is a most beautiful tree; the young dark brown twigs have a purple sheen and the bottom of the trunk carries contrasting black patches.

Morphology. Silver birch has characteristics that make it unmistakable: its milk-white trunk; a bark that sheds a thin papery skin (cracked at the base only in older trees); and its sparse, thin crown, which moves in the slightest breeze. The leaves are rhomboid, pointed, doubly notched, carried on long petioles, and attached to strong, slender branches.

Varieties. Nurserymen sometimes call this tree by the Linnaean name *Betula alba*, a collective species that was later divided into *B. pendula*, *B. pubescens*, distinguished by smooth twigs and ovate, pubescent leaves, and *B. papyrifera*, the paper birch. For the same reason, it is incorrect to use *B. alba pendula* to indicate forms with particularly drooping branches. These are, instead, *B. pendula* var. *tristis*, with rather thin branches hanging straight down, and var. *gracilis*, which is similar, but with less abundant foliage.

A decorative effect is achieved by the variety *purpurea*, with dark red leaves bronze-green in autumn. The variety *dalecarlica* has pointed leaves, somewhat triangular and deeply lobed. Variety *fastigiata* has a columnar habit similar to the Lombardy poplar.

In North East America *B. nigra*, the River Birch, produces fine specimens up to 60 feet. It has a shaggy cream-coloured trunk and grows equally well away from water or near to it.

Origin. The birch is native to Europe and Asia, and is spread throughout the Alps up to 5,000 feet and in the moorlands of the high plains.

Cultivation. In the natural state it grows in full sun, forming sparse forests and avoiding mutual competition. It is a pioneer plant, occupying abandoned fields and pastures, and prefers an acid, moist, but well-drained soil. It tolerates extreme cold.

Since the tree gives little shade, it is grown for its aesthetic value, in small groups or copses, to highlight the autumnal golden yellow foliage against a background of green lawn. The low-density of its shade allows many bulbs and flowering plants to thrive beneath it.

The wood of some varieties is used for making bobbins, fish cakes and veneers. Trunks that have retained their bark are used in rustic fences, although they do not last. The bark is used in baskets. In some countries the sap is used in brewing birch beer.

The tree propagates easily by seed in a loose, mineral soil, covered lightly with earth. Many insects and diseases attack the leaves, the shoots, and the wood, but without epidemic effects.

62, 63. Group of *Betula pendula*, and detail with fruit.

62

Hornbeam

Carpinus Betulus, family Betulaceae
This genus name was given by the early Romans.

Morphology. It is a tree of modest size, usually not taller than 50 to 60 feet, with a trunk that is never round, but somewhat spirated, covered with a grey, fluted bark, even at an advanced age. The crown is dense and round. The alternate leaves are deciduous, oval, acute or pointed, with a serrated edge and numerous veins, dark green above, lighter underneath.

The tree is monoecious and flowers appear in spring together with the leaves. The males are pendant catkins, about an inch long; the females are shorter and less conspicuous, but develop a much showier fruit of trilobed leafy bracts surrounding small achene-like nuts.

Varieties. Horticultural varieties include *asplenifolia*, cut-leaved, *japonica*, of sturdy pyramidal habit, and *pendula* with long weeping branches. Native to China is *C. Turczaninovii* var. *ovalifolia*, of graceful habit and tinted young growths, that reaches 25 feet.

Cultivation. *Carpinus Betulus* is a forest tree native to Europe and western Asia, rather shade-loving, typical of mixed hardwood forests of the plains and hills having plentiful rainfall and a fertile, acid soil. It is a slow-growing plant with a short life.

This tree withstands severe pruning well and is useful to form green arches, high hedges and screens which take on a yellow colour in the autumn.

Propagation is by seed. Branches that touch the earth may root. If plants are to be used in hedges, seedlings must be transplanted at the end of the first year and well spaced in order to obtain vigorous trees. The varieties are propagated by grafting on the species.

The hornbeam is injured by early frost in autumn or in late spring; sudden and excessive changes in temperature may cause damage. *C. caroliniana*, known as American Hornbeam, is similar to *C. Betulus*.

64, 65. Male and female flowers of *Carpinus Betulus*.

66, 67. Branch with fruit and detail of leaves and fruit of *Carpinus Betulus*.

68

72

69

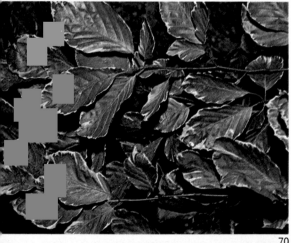

70

73

71

Beech

Fagus sylvatica, family Fagaceae
The generic name is taken from the Latin, while the species name recalls the forest habitat.

Morphology. The Common beech is a broad-leaved tree of an imposing habit, up to 100 feet tall. It has a smooth ash-grey bark with a hemispherical form in isolated specimens and dense foliage.

Leaves are alternate, oval or elliptical, pointed, entire or almost so, wavy at the edges, dark green and shiny on top, lighter and dull beneath, rust-coloured when dry, and sometimes persist on the tree for much of the winter.

The male flowers are pendulous heads, and the females are in pairs in an axillary involucre. They bloom in spring as the leaves appear; the seeds (beechnuts) are brown three-angled nuts. It is a gregarious tree and so is frequently found in small groups or making up much of an expansive woodland. If in competition with other species it is likely to emerge dominant because its roots take fairly rapidly to the top soil.

Varieties. Some varieties of beech are widely grown in parks. Especially noteworthy among these are: *atropunicea*, the Copper beech with dark red leaves; *laciniata*, the Cutleaf beech; *asplenifolia*; *pendula*, the Weeping beech with

74

75

branches reaching to the ground; *purpurea*, the Purple beech; *tricolor* with whitish leaves dotted with green and edged with pink.

Origin. The Common Beech is native to Britain, and to Central and Southern Europe where it is found in Alpine and Appenine valleys from 2,500 to 6,000 feet up.

Cultivation. It prefers a well-drained soil of limestone origin but grows well in acid soil provided it is not overleached. The beech is suitable for large parks, assuming a quite massive size, and is also a good seaside tree. For good growth, it needs much open space around it.

The ornamental varieties are propagated by grafts on the species, ordinarily in the greenhouse in early spring; because of the heavy water requirements of the plant, grafts in the open do not ordinarily give good results. The seeds, which are difficult to keep, are sown one inch deep in March or April in rows 15 inches apart. Gun stocks, joiners' tools and the curved portions of wooden wheels are made from the timber.

68. Branch and fruit of *Fagus sylvatica*.

69, 70. Variously coloured leaves of *Fagus sylvatica* var. *tricolor*.

71. Incised leaves of *Fagus sylvatica* var. *asplenifolia*.

72. Prostrate shape of *Fagus sylvatica* var. *pendula*.

73. Crown of *Fagus sylvatica* var. *purpurea*.

Plane tree

Platanus acerifolia, family Platanaceae
The genus derives from its ancient Greek name. The name acerifolia refers to the resemblance of its leaves to those of the maples. The tree is frequently and incorrectly called sycamore. This species is the London plane tree.

Origin. This tree is considered by most botanists to be a hybrid between *Platanus orientalis*, of the Balkans and Asia Minor, and *P. occidentalis*, of North America, but some believe it to be a mutation of *P. orientalis*. It is the plane tree most commonly grown in Europe. In America, *P. occidentalis* is the more common. Several London squares retain the plane trees originally laid out in the eighteenth century, Berkeley Square and Lincoln's Inn Fields being good examples.

Morphology. This tree may reach 100 feet in height. It has a robust habit, a trunk often thickened at the base and covered with a particular kind of bark, scaly in the lower parts and shedding in thin plates producing vari-coloured pastel tones ranging from cream-white through greenish to light brown, leaving the trunk almost smooth. The branches are thick and form a more or less globular crown, which gives good shade. The leaves are deciduous, petioled, palmate with 3 to 5 lobes and prominent veins. They are variable in form, and intermediate between those of the two parents; the leaves are more sharply subdivided in the oriental plane tree and have very shallow lobes in the American plane tree.

The small male and female flowers (the tree is monoecious) are similar to each other, but on separate peduncles; the fruit is pendant, spherical, and persistent during winter. In spring the fruit releases the small seeds, each with long reddish hairs that facilitate dissemination.

Varieties. Two varieties with variegated leaves exist, *Suttneri*, variegated white, and *Kelseyana*, yellow. A third variety, *pyramidalis*, is of pyramidal habit. *P. occidentalis*, the Buttonwood or American plane, grows to 150 feet in southern parts of the U.S.A. but is seldom seen in Britain.

Cultivation. The plane tree succeeds best in deep, cool soil, but is rather adaptable, surviving even with asphalt up to its base; it prefers full sun, is resistant to cold, and is somewhat resistant to air pollutants. Dry soil is unsuitable.

The plane is good as a street tree and along highways. It is valued for its hardiness, its adaptability to pruning and shaping, and for the decorativeness of its foliage and bark.

The wood of the tree, rather heavy and hard, ordinarily has little value.

It is propagated by seed protected from direct sun; after two years it is transplanted. It may be propagated by cuttings taken from mature branches with a spur, in June or later, under glass, and this is the method generally recommended as the tree often does not set fertile seed. Developed specimens may be moved easily.

74. *Platanus acerifolia* in autumn.

75. Scaly bark of *Platanus acerifolia*.

Sweet gum

Liquidambar Styraciflua, family Hamamelidaceae
The name of the genus means "liquid amber" in Latin because of the sap produced by the tree, and is recalled in the species name composed of a Greek word, "styrax", and the Latin "fluere", to secrete. The common name is Sweet Gum.

Morphology. This tree, of smaller size in cultivation, exceeds 100 feet in nature. It has a regular, dense crown, spreading if isolated, and a brown-grey trunk with bark deeply fissured longitudinally. The branches develop corky wings. Leaves are alternate, deciduous, palmate, with 5 to 7 triangular lobes somewhat star shaped and minutely serrated, shiny on top, dull and lighter underneath with a long petiole. They have the odour of balsam if crushed.

The flowers are small and devoid of petals; the males in spikes, the females in heads. The fruit is formed towards the end of summer on a long peduncle and is a dense, spherical head of compact capsules, persisting through the winter. The seeds are winged.

Varieties. There exists a choice form in California by the name Palo Alto, which develops an orange-red leaf colour in the autumn. There are also varieties *formosana*, growing from 60 to 80 feet, and *orientalis*. In Britain the trees do not attain the maximum height.

Origin. *L. Styraciflua* is native to the U.S., *L. formosana* originated in China and *L. orientalis* in Asia Minor.

Cultivation. In its natural state it is found in forests and in the damp soil along rivers that is flooded part of the year but not swampy. In cultivation it needs cool soil and full exposure to the sun; it tolerates cold to about —5°F. Growth is slow but the tree is long-lived. In Britain it rarely exceeds half of its height in the wild.

The Sweet Gum has handsome autumnal tints in its foliage, usually red-crimson, sometimes golden-yellow or orange-red.

The aromatic resin, extracted by incision of the trunk, was once used in the manufacture of chewing gum and contains compounds of cinnamic acid and an essential oil; the balm is listed in pharmocopoeia as a curative for certain diseases of the skin and is used in perfumes as a fixative. The timber is used chiefly for panelling. The sapwood and heartwood have different names commercially; the former is hazel pine, the latter satin walnut and red gum.

Propagation is by seed sown for horticultural purposes $\frac{1}{8}$ inch deep in sandy soil outdoors. The seed is stratified as soon as mature; most seed will not germinate until the second year. Cuttings of new growth roots will do well if planted in the autumn. At time of transplantation the plant should be pruned to enhance survival.

---

76. Leaf detail of *Liquidambar Styraciflua*.

77. Branch of *Liquidambar Styraciflua* with palmate leaves, here shown in early autumn.

78. *Celtis australis*.

76

Hackberry

Celtis australis, family Ulmaceae
The name *Celtis* was in use among the Romans centuries ago.

Morphology. This is a tall tree, often referred to as the Nettle Tree, that grows up to 70 feet, with a vigorous trunk that is grooved or somewhat warty, greyish, with strong limbs and thin branches. The crown is dense and globular, with deciduous, oval-lanceolate leaves, sharply pointed at the tip, thick, veined, dark green and rough on top, grey-green and downy beneath.

The flowers are small and inconspicuous; the stone fruits, on a peduncle, are almost spherical, about the size of peas, violet-black, with a large, wrinkled nut and a sweetish pulp, sought by the birds.

The root system is foraging and permits the tree to grow in rock clefts and among boulders and in drought areas. Growth is relatively slow but the tree is long-lived, up to 300 years and more.

Origin. *Celtis australis* is native to Southern Europe, Northern Africa, and Western Asia, and in warm areas can be found at an altitude of 3,000 feet.

Cultivation. It is essentially sun-loving, yet its hardy character makes it adaptable to rocky, dry soil. When young, it may be injured by severe freezing, but later tolerates —5°F cold.

It is used in reforestation as a preparatory species in poor soil. At one time it was cultivated for its branches, which are flexible and were used for making whip handles. The wood is tough and springy and has some use for tools and carriage making. The fruit is edible and laxative; the flowers attract bees.

This tree is sometimes employed to form shady lanes because of its hardiness and the good shade it furnishes.

Propagation is by planting mature seeds in spring; after 2 to 3 years the seedlings may be transplanted with ease. Shoots can be layered in spring or autumn. Ordinary soil is suitable. The tree likes a position in a sunny shrubbery where it should be planted from October to February.

Other species. *C. occidentalis* is the native American tree, generally with broader leaves, and orange-red to dark purple fruit. It is more resistant to cold than the European species, and grows up to 130 feet.

C. Bungeana, native to Northern China reaches 25 feet. Another species native to the southern states of America is *C. laevigata* (sometimes called *C. mississippiensis*) that grows to 60 feet and has long narrow leaves.

79

Magnolia

Magnolia grandiflora, family Magnoliaceae
The genus Magnolia is named after Pierre Magnol, director of the Botanic Garden at Montpelier. The species term refers to the size of the flower, which reaches diameters of 8 to 12 inches. It was first seen in Britain in 1734.

Morphology. This is an evergreen tree, with an ovoid or conical-cylindrical crown, with a smooth, grey bark, about 15 to 20 feet tall in Britain, but in the swamp lands of America has occasionally reached 100 feet. The leaves are alternate, large, narrowly elliptical to ovate, entire, thick, leathery, with a pointed tip and wedge-shaped base. They are from 3 to 4 inches

08

81

82

83

84

long and 1 or 2 inches wide, shiny on top, dull and lighter or rust-coloured underneath, with edges curved in towards the underside.

Flowers are white, with 6 to 12 concave, large, white petals that are fragrant; they appear from May to September according to district, May flowers being seen only in the warmest areas. The fruit is an ovate cone covered with rusty down; the seeds are in a coral-red covering, although in Britain these cones are rarely borne.

Varieties. The known varieties differ little from the species (*lanceolata, gloriosa, rotundifolia* and *gallissouiensis*).

Origin. This is the only magnolia with evergreen leaves that is widely grown; it grows naturally in the humid plains of the Gulf of Mexico and along the U.S. Atlantic coast, where it tolerates flooding if not too prolonged.

Cultivation. This plant prefers an acid, fertile, and cool soil and ample space must be provided. It is resistant to 0° or −5°F but hard frost, rapid decreases in temperature, and strong winds may cause damage to leaves and branches.

This tree is best when grown as a specimen, and is of value for its shiny foliage and for its showy and prolonged flowering.

It is propagated by seed, which must be fully ripe and stratified in moist soil or sand until spring. The resinous aril is removed before storage. It is sown in the greenhouse and transplanted to pots at the appearance of true leaves; in July it is transplanted to a larger pot, and the specimen is ready to plant in its permanent position the following year; it is best to use young plants with a ball of soil to ensure their survival. Varieties are propagated by grafting. The plant can be pruned to maintain a full, dense crown.

Other species. Many deciduous magnolias are grown for their short but spectacular spring bloom, showier than *grandiflora* because of the absence of foliage.

Magnolia denudata, from China, is a tree that may reach 30 feet, with large, bell-shaped, white flowers, and obovate leaves. *M. liliflora*, from China and Japan, is sometimes designated *M. purpurea* because of the colour of the flowers.

M. Sieboldi, from Japan and Korea, grows to 30 feet, has white, fragrant flowers in the shape of a cup which appear with the leaves.

M. Soulangeana, a hybrid between *M. denudata* and *M. liliflora*, has precocious flowers, white inside and purple outside, with obovate or obovate-oblong leaves. This species and *M. stellata* are suitable for greenhouse culture.

M. stellata is shrubby and has an extravagant white display of star-shaped flowers (rosy in one variety), before the leaves appear.

---

79. *Magnolia liliflora*, in bloom.

80. Corolla of *Magnolia grandiflora*.

81, 84. *Magnolia Soulangeana* and detail of the flower.

82, 83. *Magnolia stellata* in bloom and detail of the flower.

85

Tulip tree

Liriodendron Tulipifera, family Magnoliaceae
The generic name is from two Greek words, *lyrion* (lily) and *dendron* (tree) since the flowers appear something like certain species of lilies; *tulipifera* means "tulip-bearing", an attempt to establish a relationship between the two flowers. It was first introduced into Britain in the mid-seventeenth century.

Morphology. The tulip tree is majestic, growing from 100 to 135 feet high, with a cylindrical, erect trunk and grey bark deeply fissured longitudinally. It has upright limbs with the branches more or less arched downwards. The tree has an oval, sparse form.

The deciduous leaves are of a particular form —the side lobes are pointed, separated from the central third lobe by a wide gap; the latter is truncated and incised at the centre; the petiole is long, the upper surface bluish-green, somewhat shiny, the lower surface lighter and dull. In autumn they turn to gold.

The flowers, lightly fragrant, open in May and June after the leaves, and are about 2 inches in diameter, are erect, in the shape of a conch shell, consisting of 6 light yellow-green petals with orange spots on the outside. The fruit is cone shaped and contains numerous samaras, each with a lanceolate wing that becomes free in the autumn; the axil of the fruit persists on the tree.

Varieties. The following varieties are to be noted: *fastigiatum*, narrow pyramid form; *integrifolium*, with lobeless leaves; *aureomaculatum*, with gold-mottled leaves.

Origin. The tulip tree is a forest plant of alluvial, sandy, damp but well-drained soil, native to the U.S. from Massachusetts to Florida and Mississippi, where it grows alone or mixed with other broadleaves.

Cultivation. This is a sun-loving species, and needs light and space. It is resistant to cold (some specimens have resisted as low as −20°F). Growth is rapid; the tree may live for 300 years.

It is used as a specimen tree in parks, or in rows; it is remarkable when in flower and when the foliage turns to brown and gold in autumn.

The wood, light and soft, has many uses, for plywood, furniture, carpentry, and pulp. At one time the inside of the bark, bitter with the presence of liriodendrin, was used as a tonic. The tree is frequently and erroneously called "poplar".

Propagation is by seed sown in autumn or by layering in spring; varieties are grafted or propagated cuttings. Transplanting is tenuous because the fleshy roots dry rapidly in the sun and should be done in spring.

---

85. Tulip-tree in autumn.

86. *Liriodendron Tulipifera* with flower and leaves.

86

Tamarisk

Tamarix gallica, family Tamaricaceae
The generic name of this tree was in use among the Romans; the term *gallica* indicates the plant was first found in Gaul, now known as France. The common name is Tamarisk. It comes from the Hebrew word *tamaris* meaning a sweeping broom and the foliage is certainly broom-like.

Morphology. Tamarisk is a shrub or small tree, 10 to 30 feet high, with long, slender, weak, curved twigs. The brown or reddish-brown bark is covered with numerous plump lenticels in a series of rings; the bark fissures only at advanced age. The leaves are very small, blue-green, rhombic-ovate, sheathed, close together, half-embracing the stem, semitransparent and smooth.

Flowers appear from May to July; they are small but numerous, grouped in cylindrical racemes above and around the branches and form large panicles. There are 5 pale rose petals; the fruit is a three-sided capsule containing seeds having a tuft of hairs at the tip.

Varieties. *T. anglica*, the Common Tamarisk with white and pink flowers, is an evergreen like *T. gallica*, and is native to Britain. *T. gallica*, var. *mannifera* native to Asia Minor, provides a white honey-like secretion that is eaten by desert-dwellers in those areas.

Cultivation. Tamarisk is a typical halophyte species (literally, salt-loving) that thrives on damp shores tolerating brackish water and salt spray. It is also suited to soil that is extremely calcareous, compacted, and poorly aerated, or to beach sand where it is often used to shore up landslides and coastal dunes because of its rapid spread. While thriving on seashores, it is resistant to cold to −5°F. It is frequently used as a low windbreak.

In gardens south of the Trent it is grown as specimen near water, or in hedges, and is particularly ornamental during flowering.

The wood of tamarisk, subject to splitting and twisting, has no particular value. The bark is rich in tannin.

It may be propagated by seed, which should be barely covered with soil or, more often, by cuttings of mature or green wood. To obtain a good growth of new branches, it is necessary to prune lightly.

Other species. Rather numerous (75 to 80) and difficult to distinguish are the deciduous species of tamarisk of western Europe, the Mediterranean region, and western Asia. Among those grown as ornamentals are *Tamarix pentandra* and *T. parviflora*, the latter often confused with *T. africana*. *T. parviflora* flowers earlier, in May. *T. pentandra* flowers late.

T. hispida, a rather tender species native to the Caspian area, has pink flowers and glaucous foliage.

Fungi that attack the tamarisk cause disease of the leaves and root rot or stem rot.

---

87. The abundant flowering of a tamarisk.

88. *Tamarix pentandra*.

87

88

Flowering plums, cherries, almonds

Genus *Prunus*, family Rosaceae
Prunus is the Latin name for this genus. Here we describe some of its ornamental species.

Different species. *Prunus serrulata* (flowering cherry) is one of the most beautiful flowering trees we can grow, singly or in rows. It is native to China, Korea, and Japan and has numerous varieties, some with double flowers. These are almost all of Japanese origin. It is generally grown as a standard, making a tree from 15 to 30 feet. The chestnut-coloured bark flakes in concentric circles like the fruiting trees, and its bearing is similar. The leaves are oval, ovate, or obovate, pointed, smooth, somewhat blue-green and glaucous underneath, and toothed. The flowers have no fragrance, are white or rose in great profusion in early spring at leafing or just before, and are grouped in clusters of five to seven.

It is propagated by budding on *P. cerasifera* var. *atropurpurea*, the purple-leaved plum. This tree is not normally pruned. It has no particular soil requirements, and its hardiness depends on the variety. Its common name is Kwanzan. Another variety, *P. serrulata erecta* or Amanagowa, is excellent for terraces where space is limited. From a low root stock it establishes itself as a slender upright column of one or more slim stems bearing semi-double pink blossoms.

89

90

91

92

93

Prunus japonica is a dwarf, flowering cherry, a shrubby type up to 4 feet in height, and in the variety *flore pleno* grown for its magnificent, rosy, double flowers which precede the leaves and densely cover the branches. The fruit is wine-red. This dwarf variety is a good garden plant and is commercially grown on a large scale.

P. triloba, also known as flowering almond, is a fine shrub indigenous to China. It responds best if treated as a climber. *P. triloba* var. *plena* is suitable for forcing in the greenhouse, is double flowered, and does not produce fruit.

Fruit is also rather rare in the single-flowering forms. The species name comes from the leaf shape, divided into three at the tip, widely ovate or obovate, sharply pointed, deeply and doubly serrated. The flowers are solitary on a short pedicel, are bright pink, and appear in spring with the foliage. It likes lime in the soil, and is propagated by grafting on plums which produces short-lived plants; propagation by division or root grafting on the plum is considered best. The variety *Petzoldii* does not have tri-lobed leaves.

For spots of colour and low hedges, *P. cerasifera* var. *atropurpurea* is also used. This shrub has purple-red leaves and blooms after the leaves appear in spring. It has small rosy flowers, barely visible. The fruit is spherical and red with an edible sweet-sour pulp. This tree is also resistant to cold. The typical flowering *Prunus* trees have green leaves; the purple-leaved plum is used as a rootstock for flowering cherries, as are *P. Cerasus* (sour cherry) and *P. avium* (sweet cherry).

---

89. *Prunus serrulata* (Japanese flowering cherry).

90. *Prunus triloba*.

91. *Prunus subhirtella* var. *pendula* (Rosebud cherry).

92. *Prunus cerasifera* cultivar Highan (Cherry or Myrobalan plum).

93. *Malus floribunda* (showy Crab Apple).

Mimosa and acacia

Albizzia = Acacia Julibrissin, family Leguminosae

Morphology. The mimosa is a small tree, 25 to 35 feet tall, with the spreading habit of the acacias, branches somewhat horizontal, forming a flat top. The branches are sparse and create a silky appearance because of the finely subdivided bipinnate leaves. Each leaf has 9 to 12 pairs of pinnae.

The flowers appear during July and August and are groups of heads in terminal clusters. They have no petals and are comprised of many long, diverging stamens, of a rosy colour. The trunk and limbs are devoid of spines.

Origin. This species, native to dry areas from Iran to Japan, needs full light and well-drained soil; it will not tolerate severe cold, and is not hardy in the open through the British winter.

Cultivation. The albizzia is used best as a specimen, and is very popular because of the airiness of the foliage and the showy bloom. It is sensitive to cold, is ravaged by web-worm, and is susceptible to the soil-borne verticillium wilt, which usually causes death.

Other species. Closely related to this tree are the acacias (genus *Acacia*), which are grown for cut flowers and for ornament in Mediterranean gardens and to create shady lanes. This genus is native to the dry regions of Australia, Africa and Asia, where it forms arboreal savannahs and sparse forests. In Britain it is usually treated as a greenhouse flowering shrub or small tree.

Many of the cultivated kinds vary in being either evergreen or deciduous, having either bipinnate leaves or leaves reduced to leaf-like petioles, being either tall trees or low shrubs, and being either spineless or free of spines. All, however, have small flowers that appear in late winter or early spring, with reduced petals while the long stamens form heads in large clusters, resembling golden-yellow or white wads of cotton.

Most species are grown for the flowers; others, high in tannin and having a rapid growth rate, are used in warm countries as vegetation for sand dunes to arrest shifting sand and to serve as windbreak in frost free areas. All the mimosas prefer full sun.

Propagation is by seed, but the seed-bed temperature must be kept above 60°F. Germination can be hastened by treating the seed with boiling water before sowing. If the seeds are old, this is done more than once.

Transplanting is difficult because of the long tap root; it is therefore preferable to sow in containers and transplant the seedling while very young. The ornamental types are propagated by approach grafting on *Acacia retinodes* in summer. After flowering, which occurs at the end of winter, they should be pruned to encourage thick crowns and prevent fruiting, which is not ornamental.

Acacias are also injured by hard freezing and will not tolerate temperatures below 20°F.

Various insects may damage acacias in their native habitat and where it has been cultivated for centuries, as in South Africa, for example, where it is grown for the production of tannin.

The species most grown for ornament are *A. decurrens*; *A. longifolia*; *A. Farnesiana*, used for the making of perfume; *A. podalyriaefolia*; *A. cultriformis*; *A. spectabilis*; *A. Baileyana*.

---

94. *Albizzia julibrissin.*

95. Close-up of *Albizzia julibrissin.*

96. Inflorescence of an acacia.

97. *Acacia Farnesiana.*

98

Redbud or judas tree

Cercis Siliquastrum, family Cesalpiniaceae
The   name derives from the legend that Judas hanged himself on this tree after betraying Christ.

Morphology. This is a deciduous tree or shrub, growing from 15 to 40 feet, with a trunk often twisted and branching down to the ground, covered with a blackish bark, extremely rough because of transverse and longitudinal cracking. The crown is broad and leggy; the leaves, round, heart-shaped, smooth, dark green on the upper surface, lighter below, on a long petiole.

Redbud flowers early in spring. The butterfly-shaped flowers are rose-lilac, and appear on the trunk, limbs and branches in thick clusters, in vivid contrast to the dark limbs and to the sprouting leaves. The fruit is a compressed pod, reddish and persistent. This tree is generally considered to be the best garden species.

Varieties. Variety *alba* has white flowers.

Origin. *C. Siliquastrum* is native to southern Europe and western Asia where it grows to an altitude of 3,000 feet. It was first introduced into Britain in the late sixteenth century.

Cercis canadensis, the American Redbud, is native to the United States from Connecticut and Pennsylvania to Michigan, west to Missouri, south to Texas and Florida. It grows to between 15 and 40 feet, and is similar in appearance and growth to *C. Siliquastrum*. The Chinese Redbud, *C. chinensis*, is potentially a small tree but in most landscape plantings is grown as a shrub.

Cultivation. *C. Siliquastrum* has a rather slow growth. It adapts well to most soil types. In the north of England grow it against a south wall.

Redbud is suited for street plantings and is grown for its attractive flowers and leaves and for its resistance to air pollutants. It may be forced in the greenhouse for cut flowers. Its wood is used for small pieces and inlay work. The flowers may be eaten in salads.

Propagation is by seed; cuttings may also be taken during September and October. Redbud is attacked by some diseases: a canker, some leaf-spots, a root rot, and two sapwood rots.

---

98. *Cercis Siliquastrum* in bloom.

99

100

Japanese pagoda tree

Sophora japonica, family Leguminosae
The name of the genus seems to be derived from the Arabic name, *sophero*, for a tree with pea-shaped flowers; the name of the species shows that the tree originated in Japan. It was introduced into Britain in the middle of the eighteenth century.

Morphology. In the type species this is a tree of rather lofty stature (65 to 80 feet), with a broad rounded crown, not very dense, with a straight cylindrical trunk having a grey bark slightly fissured longitudinally.

The limbs are broad and twisted; the branches are slender, shiny, and are green. The deciduous leaves are unequally pinnate, with 7 to 17 oval-acute, entire, smooth, dark green leaflets, shiny on top and blue-green underneath.

It blooms in August and September, depending on temperature, in large, loose, terminal panicles, with yellowish white butterfly-like flowers having a pleasing aroma. The pod, about an inch long, resembles a string of beads.

Varieties. Among the varieties, there is *violacea* whose flower has both purplish wings and keel and whose leaves are densely hairy underneath.

S. japonica var. *pendula* is a smaller tree, growing to about 30 feet, and because of its weeping habit it must be grafted high (at least 6 feet) on a trunk of the type species. The limbs are extremely twisted in rather bizarre forms, while the thin branches are pendent but not very broad; in all, with time, a rather picturesque crown will

form, which is assisted by judicious and not excessive pruning.

Cultivation. *Sophora* is adapted to most soils, provided they are deep and well drained. It needs a warm position in full sun and wall protection except in the Cornish riviera. Despite the name, in Japan the species grows only under cultivation; it is native to China and Korea.

The typical Japanese pagoda tree does not give much shade, but for its hardiness and the interesting foliage it is useful in groves and lanes. The variety *pendula* is good as a specimen tree, and the variety *variegata* has leaves margined with creamy white. Almost all parts of the plant are purgative. The flowers are visited by bees.

The typical species is propagated by seed sown in spring; the varieties by grafting on the type. *Sophora* is rarely attacked by insects; among diseases there is a wilt of the stem shoots and a root rot. Excessive pruning is harmful.

Other species. Plants of another family with a habit similar to that of the variety *pendula* (but with branches less twisted) include European Ash (*Fraxinus excelsior* var. *pendula*) and white mulberry (*Morus alba* var. *pendula*).

---

99. The typical crown of *Sophora japonica* var. *pendula*.

100. The mulberry (*Morus alba*) often has a decorative effect.

Sycamore maple

Acer Pseudo-Platanus, family Aceraceae
The name *Acer* was in use among the early Romans; the species name refers to the slight resemblance of the leaves to the plane tree.

Morphology. This tree is majestic and will attain 100 feet. It has a large, straight trunk and a dense, rather rounded top especially in isolated specimens. The bark on young trees is smooth and grey; later, scales develop that drop off gradually.

The leaves are deciduous, opposite, on a rather long petiole, large, palmate with five broadly wedge-shaped lobes deeply divided with unequally toothed edges green and shiny on top, blue-green and dull underneath, where the veining stands out in sharp relief.

The small greenish flowers, in drooping panicles, appear in April or May. The double samaras are showy, have two oval seeds, each attached to a membranous, oblong, arching wing. The two wings compose a right angle and facilitate dissemination; the wind gives them a spiral motion and carries them some distance.

Varieties. Among the varieties, those with coloured leaves are of some interest: *erythrocarpum* has shiny leaves and red fruits; *purpureum* has leaves that are purple underneath; *Worleei* has yellow leaves and a red petiole; *variegatum* has variegated leaves dotted with white; and others. *Leopoldii* is suitable for small gardens as it is slow-growing and *Handjeryi* is extremely slow-growing.

101

103

102

104

105

Origin. Sycamore maple is a rare tree occurring mixed with other broadleaves up to an altitude of 5,000 feet in the wild.

Cultivation. It thrives on various soils if not too compact. It prefers full sun, although it tolerates shade when young. In culture it does not have particular requirements. It grows rapidly and will live from 500 to 700 years.

It is used for shady lanes because of its vigour and the shade given by the top, while isolated specimens create an interesting effect, especially in autumn when the leaves acquire a warm golden-yellow colour.

Propagation is by seed; the varieties are grafted in summer. Leaves are disfigured by spots caused by a fungus, *Rhytisma acerinum*.

Other species. *Acer platanoides* (Norway maple) recognizable by the rather acute tips of its leaf lobes, grows up to 50 feet in height.

The box elder (*A. Negundo*) is widely grown for its wide adaptation. Forms with variegated leaves are of particular interest. It may be used in small plantings, tolerates pruning, but is subject to wind breakage.

---

101. Flowering branches of *Acer Pseudo-Platanus*.

102, 104. *Acer Negundo* with variegated leaves, and a flowering branch.

103. *Acer platanoides* cultivar "Fassen's black".

105. Detail of the foliage of *Sophora japonica* var. *pendula*.

106

107

108

109

110

111

Japanese maple

Acer palmatum, family Aceraceae
The species name refers to the leaf shapes which appear in numerous forms. The tree has spread throughout the world because of the aesthetic value of the various cultivars that originated in Japan and Korea, each distinguished by a local name.

Morphology. This is a shrub or small tree, 25 feet or less, that acquires a picturesque and "Japanese" look with its thick, twisted trunk, branching from the base. The trunk is smooth and greyish and the crown is dense and spreading. The leaves are small and smooth, palmate, with 5 to 9 sharp lobes, in varied forms and colours among the varieties. Varieties vary in form: fully-leaved limbs to those with leaves on only a third of the limb; lobes vary from linear to broad; edges may be incised, toothed, or almost entire. As to colour, leaves may be of a single shade or of varied colours: green, red, completely purple, or any of these, with edges in carmine, yellow, green with white spots, green with a rosy border, yellow green with dark green borders and veins, spotted with white, pink, or red, etc.; the different forms and colours of the leaves combine variously together. The colours, furthermore, vary considerably during the year, with delicate pastel tints in spring when the leaves develop, while in autumn the colours become more intense; even the green types acquire rosy or red, yellow or orange shades in autumn.

The flowers, small and purplish, are in erect

112

113

114

115

Horse chestnut or buckeye

corymbs; the fruits, as in other maples, are double-winged in an obtuse angle.

Cultivation. The soil should be fertile, slightly acid, and well drained. It is a slow-growing species of great horticultural interest, valued for the elegant, light foliage and the various colourations it may acquire. Because of its small size, it lends itself well in warm areas to gardens on terraces and balconies, grown in tubs. Otherwise it should be potted in a cool greenhouse.

The varieties are propagated by grafting in March, by layering in October, or by budding for the choice Japanese kinds in August. Seeds can be sown $\frac{1}{4}$ inch deep in October.

Other species. Another maple of the same origin, *Acer japonicum*, is often grown under the same common name. It is distinguished by leaves with 9 to 11 small lobes and deeply-toothed edges.

---

106. *Acer palmatum*, with purple leaves.

107. *Acer japonicum*.

108. Bronze form of *Acer palmatum* with heavily subdivided leaves.

109. *Acer palmatum* in spring.

110. Foliage of *Acer palmatum*.

111. *Acer palmatum*, cultivar "Koko".

Aesculus Hippocastanum, family Hippocastanaceae

In classical Latin the name *aesculus* indicated a kind of oak; the fruit of this tree, resembling chestnuts, was believed to cure diseases of the horse. It was described in 1557 by Mattioli and around the beginning of the seventeenth century was widely used at Versailles; it was extensively planted by Cardinal Richelieu and used a great deal by Le Notre in his gardens *a la francaise*.

Morphology. This tree, reaching 100 feet, is characterized by its robust trunk covered with scaly grey-brown bark, and for the compact crown, and thick, almost erect, limbs. The leaves are opposite, digitate-palmate, with 5 to 7 sessile leaflets, wedge-shaped at the base and rounded to a point at the tip, and doubly toothed.

The flowers are very showy, composed of 5 wavy, white petals, spotted with red, in erect terminal panicles. The fruits are large, spherical, and spiny, and contain 1 to 3 large, round, or hemispherical, shiny reddish-brown seeds with a pale hilar scar.

Varieties. Varieties include *luteovariegata*, *variegata*, *incisa*, *laciniata*, *pyramidalis*; the variety *Baumannii* has double, sterile, white flowers. An interesting form is *A. carnea*, a hybrid of *A. Hippocastanum* and *A. Pavia*, which combines the height of the female parent with the red flower colour of the male. *A. turbinata* is the creamy Japanese Horse Chestnut.

Cultivation. This is a tree that readily propagates by seed. It will tolerate temperatures as low as 15 to 20 degrees below zero. Although not particularly associated with any one type of soil, it prospers in cool, fertile soil and does not grow well in damp or dry or compacted soil.

The tree is commonly used as an ornamental, either isolated or in groups, especially to make shady lanes where it is appreciated for its early leafing, the beautiful spring bloom, and its dense shade; it is not often planted as a forest tree. The wood is used for fencing, packing cases and carving. The fruit, rather rich in starch, is bitter because of its saponin content which produces a lather and thus may be used as a detergent.

Horse chestnut seed may be planted in spring after winter stratifications; in one or two years seedlings are transplanted. Varieties are grafted in March or budded in July.

It is subject to very little insect damage, but older specimens are hollowed out by wood rotting fungi; disease spots may appear on the leaves. Pollution can cause early loss of leaves.

Other species. The hybrid of the American *A. Pavia* (with thornless fruit) and the common horse chestnut is preferred as it is more rugged and capable of attaining a greater size.

112, 114 *Aesculus Hippocastanum* and inflorescence.

113, 115. *Aesculus carnea* and inflorescence.

Silver linden

Tilia tomentosa = T. argentea, family Tiliaceae
Tilia is the classical Latin name; both species'
names refer to the appearance of the underside
of the leaves, which, being covered with dense
down, seem silvery white.

Morphology. This is a tree some 75 to 100 feet
tall with a sturdy structure, a dense, rounded
oval crown, a dark grey bark with only sparse,
shallow fissures. The limbs are numerous and
erect, the branches spreading, the new twigs
downy. The deciduous leaves are alternate,
large, characteristically heart-shaped, slightly
pointed, serrated, and thick with many veins.

The inflorescence, as in other lindens, consists
of drooping clusters with few flowers on each,
carried on an adnate peduncle with an obtuse,
oblong, membraneous wing, which, aided by the
wind, enhances, dissemination of the fruit. The
flowers have five yellow petals, are very fragrant
with a sweet perfume, and appear in July. The
fruit is small, ovoid, hairy, woody, and ribbed.

Varieties. *T. tomentosa* var. *pendula* is a weeping form of silver linden and is sometimes
confused with *T. petiolaris*.

Origin. The silver linden is native to southeastern Europe and western Asia.

Cultivation. It is the most hardy of the genus,
and has no preference as to soil; it tolerates
drought better than any other species of linden.
Growth is relatively rapid.

The linden is considered ornamental because
of the contrast of colours of the two sides of the
leaves, especially visible in a breeze. It is often
used for groves and lanes and specimen trees.
The strong aroma of the flowers may be annoy-
ing to some. It is not, like other lindens, honey-
producing; indeed, the nectar of *T. tomentosa*
and *T. petiolaris* may be toxic to bees.

Extracts of the flowers are used in medicine.
The wood is valuable for inlay work, toys, and
musical instruments.

Propagation is by seed gathered in autumn and
stratified in cool sand until spring, when it is
sown. Varieties are propagated by grafting in
spring or budding in summer; the resulting
specimens may have a single-stemmed crown for
some years. It is also propagated by cuttings and
by layering. Sprouts often develop from the
roots, and these may be cut off. Transplanting is
easy even for large trees.

Other species. *T. petiolaris* (Weeping White
Linden) is a weeping form similar to *T. tomentosa*
var. *pendula*; *T. platyphyllos* (Large-Leaved
Linden) has large leaves that are velvety underneath; *T. Cordata* (Small-Leaved Linden) has
small blue-green leaves, smooth on the underside
but tufted with reddish hairs at the intersections
of the veins; *T. europaea* is the hybrid of *T.
platyphyllos* and *T. cordate* is more demanding
in regard to moisture. *T. americana* (American
Linden or Basswood) is also suited for lane
planting. It has large thick leaves, light green
underneath and smooth except for a hairiness
like that on *T. Cordata*. *T. mongolica*, the
Mongolian Linden, is a graceful species.

The foliage of lindens falls early in the autumn;
it is attractive to aphids which cover the leaves
with honeydew, after which a fungus with
surface spores may develop disfiguring the leaves
with blackish spots.

116. *Tilia europaea.*

117. *Tilia cordata* in bloom.

118. Winged fruit of a linden.

119. *Tilia tomentosa.*

120, 121. Flowering panicle and leaves with fruit of
Paulownia tomentosa.

122, 123. *Catalpa bignonioides* and details of flowers.

116

118

117

119

120

121

122

Paulownia

Paulownia tomentosa, family Scrophularaceae. ariceae.

Morphology. This is a medium-sized tree, rarely as tall as 50 feet, but having a trunk of large diameter, with a grey bark. The crown is formed of thick, crooked limbs and branches and is spreading, sometimes umbrella-shaped. The deciduous leaves are opposite, large (the outer ones very large), on a long petiole, oval to heart-shaped, entire or with obtuse lobes at the sides, hairy and greyish beneath, smooth on top.

The flowers are rather showy and are initiated in the autumn preceding bloom; they open in early spring before the leaves. They are carried in erect panicles and are large, tubular, pale lilac-violet, with darker spots inside, opening at the tip in five unequal lobes arranged with two lips, in form foxglove-shaped.

The fruits are a large, rather woody, inverted pear-shaped capsule, persisting and conspicuous over winter. After being cut down, the tree regrows with great vigour from the stump, producing shoots up to 6 feet at the end of the first year, with leaves more than 20 inches long.

Varieties. Variety *lanata* has a yellow down on the underside of the leaves; variety *pallida* has pale flowers.

Origin. This tree is native to China and was introduced into Britain in the nineteenth century.

Cultivation. It prefers a deep, fertile, moist soil; it grows poorly in calcareous or dry soil. Because it continues growth unusually late in the year, the shoots that are not yet mature may be damaged by frost, and the following year's bloom may be spoiled. Woody branches can tolerate temperature as low as −5°F. It grows rapidly.

This is a fine ornamental tree, suited as a specimen and for planting in city squares and lanes because of its small size, its beautiful flowers, and the shade it affords, even though the foliage is not especially elegant.

It is propagated by seed in spring or by root-cuttings, or greenwood cuttings, sown $\frac{1}{8}$ inch deep in sandy loam in a cold frame.

Other species. *P. lilacina* is a species growing to about 50 feet. In the closely related Bignoniaceae family is a similar tree, *Catalpa bignonioides* native to the southeastern United States, which may at first sight be confused with paulownia when it is in leaf, the leaves being more or less of the same form and size in both species. Close observation, however, shows that the leaves are opposite in paulownia and in whorls of three in catalpa. The catalpa flowers are white, with yellow or red markings inside, having a broader edge and shorter tubule; the fruit is an elongated pod, 8 to 15 inches long, resembling a bean. It is also ornamental. It prefers light soil and is more hardy than paulownia. In height it ranges from 25 to 50 feet, and has an attractive variety, *aurea*.

123

124

Flowering shrubs

Chimonanthus

Chimonanthus praecox = Calycanthus praecox, family Calycanthaceae

The generic name means "winter flower", from the Greek *keimon* and *anthos*; the other generic name comes from the Latin meaning chalice because of the development of the calyx; species name refers to the earliness of flowering. It was introduced into Britain in the middle of the eighteenth century.

Morphology. This shrub grows to about 10 feet, has many stems with arching principal branches and erect secondary growth. The bark is a light grey-brown, sprinkled with numerous large lenticels like warts. The leaves are opposite, entire, oval or oblong, about 6 inches long, shiny on top, and almost sessile.

The flowers, on short, scaly twigs from the growth of the previous year, appear from December to March, depending on the temperature; they are single or in pairs, with several petal-like sepals, oval or elongated, waxy yellow and longer at the outside, veined and suffused with purple at the inside. There are 5 or 6 short stamens and many pistils. The fruit is capsule-shaped with many achene-like seeds.

Varieties. Among the varieties are *grandiflora*, with larger flowers; *concolor*, with entirely yellow flowers; *parviflorus*, with small flowers.

There is also a variety with purple flowers.

Cultivation. *Chimonanthus* is a native of China and it must be planted in a warm, sheltered position to obtain bloom in winter. It has no particular soil requirements. It is a shrub to be recommended because, in temperate climates, it is one of the very few to bloom in winter. The corollas are fragrant, with a sweet and penetrating odour that is used in making perfumes.

Propagation is by seed sown in spring, or by cuttings taken in summer, or by layering in September or October.

Other species. Another winter-flowering shrub, not widely grown, is *Hamamelis mollis*. This is an early blooming Witch Hazel that reaches a height of 10 feet, producing flowers even at low temperatures which are not damaged even if the thermometer goes below the freezing point. The bare branches are covered with aromatic flowers having four linear, twisted, golden yellow petals, and a short cup-shaped purple-red calyx. The leaves resemble hazelnut and are vividly coloured in autumn. It is propagated by seed or by layering in October or November. Grafting can be done using the stock of *H. virginiana*.

124. *Chimonanthus fragrans.*

125. *Hamamelis mollis.*

125

126

127

128

129

Hydrangeas

Genus *Hydrangea*, family Saxifragaceae
The name of the genus is from the Greek *hydor*
meaning water, and *aggeion* meaning vase,
referring thus to the cup-shaped fruit.

Morphology. There follows a complete description of the most widespread type, *Hydrangea
macrophylla*, which, according to Rehder, includes 22 principal varieties (among which is the
garden hydrangea) and numerous horticultural
forms and cultivars. *H. Hortensia* and *H.
opuloides* are older names for *H. macrophylla*.

The general characteristics of this decorative
pot species are: a shrubby bush (woody at the
base), as tall as 12 feet, with smooth stems; large
ovate to ovate-elliptical leaves, pointed or acute,
serrated; inflorescence in broad, umbrella-
shaped cymes, composed partially or entirely of
sterile flowers that have a broad calyx with four
large sepals, more or less oval, with a variable
edge and vivid colour (the fertile flowers are
small and much less conspicuous).

The flowers range from white through pink to
violet, depending somewhat on the soil pH (the
acidity-alkalinity balance) and the aluminium
content of the soil. In calcareous soil, the
varieties with violet flowers do not have this
colour at all, but are pink. The flowers appear in
June and July; the fruit is a capsule.

Origin. *H. macrophylla* is native to Japan and
China. Many varieties have been introduced
from these countries, the first coming to Britain

in the early eighteenth century.

Cultivation. The plant will not tolerate temperatures below 15°F, so that in northern areas
the tops freeze back in some winters. It prefers a
fertile, well-drained, cool soil and tolerates
shade but grows and flowers best in full sun with
adequate moisture.

It is suited for borders, groups, foundation
plantings and hedges. Types with large flowering
heads composed of sterile flowers and large,
broad, vividly-coloured sepals are grown in pots
and forced to flower in winter in the greenhouse.
They are vigorous and may be used as flowering
potted plants.

Hydrangeas are easily propagated by division
or by softwood cuttings under glass in summer.
To get large flowering heads, it is necessary to
prune rather severely each autumn or, in cold
regions, at the beginning of spring.

Many troubles afflict hydrangeas including
various diseases and insects and a nematode.

Other species. Among related species, the
panicled hydrangea, *H. paniculata*, is very
ornamental; this has small flowers, all sterile or
almost so, white (tending with time to purple),
borne in a compact, elongated florescence. It
grows to 30 feet and has thin, woody branches.
It also is grown in tubs and has requirements
similar to those of the formerly mentioned
species. It is native to China and Japan. *H.
paniculata* var. *grandiflora* (Peegee Hydrangea)

is the common outdoor hydrangea.

H. petiolaris is little known. It is native to
Japan, has many branches, a vine climbing to 50
feet, and roots easily; it has white flowers of
mixed types.

H. Sargentiana, native to China, has pale
violet flowers, large velvety leaves and grows to
6 feet. Mildew is common on hydrangeas in
Britain, especially among those grown under
glass. Brown spots with a marked red border on
the leaves is occasionally found on *H. Hortensia*.
On hydrangeas sold by florists ringspot sometimes causes lesions and distortions of the leaves.
Most varieties are resistant enough to tolerate
the disease without suffering severe damage,
although there is the possibility that some
individual plants will thereby be rendered
unsaleable. For the outdoor culture of *H.
Sargentiana* the shrub should be planted October
to November or March to April. Dead and
straggling shoots need to be pruned in March and
a top-dressing given annually. Young growth of
this variety will be injured by early spring frosts
and so needs protection. *H. paniculata* and *H.
arborescens* need annual pruning to within one
inch of the base, and free watering is called for
in dry weather. *H. xanthoneura*, also from China,
has white flowers in convex corymbs and grows
to 15 feet.

126-129. The rich bloom of *Hydrangea macrophylla*
in various colours.

130

131

132

Roses

Genus *Rosa*, family Rosaceae
Everybody is familiar with roses and their large number of forms and cultivars, continually increased by hybridization and selection by skilled floriculturists. Everyone is aware, also, of the various uses that this genus has in gardens, and it may well be said that the rose is queen of the flowering shrubs because of the large beautifully shaped flowers and range of colours.

Morphology. Roses are shrubs with erect or climbing habits, spiny, mostly with deciduous leaves; the leaves are alternate, almost always unequally pinnate, with large stipules; the flowers are borne singly or in clusters, are in diverse colours, often fragrant, composed of five petals in the natural state, becoming very numerous in doubled-types with the sexual organs also transformed into petals, and are characterized by pistils; the fruit is a red hip, fleshy when ripe.

The Greeks and Romans grew roses; indeed, the latter achieved winter flowering by forcing. The first catalogue of roses (describing 16

varieties) was published in Britain in 1597. Until the late eighteenth century only summer-flowering roses were known, while the ever-blooming types were obtained only about 1800 with the introduction of some Chinese varieties. An interesting illustrated monograph of old varieties, attractive also from an aesthetic point of view, is *Les Roses*, by P. J. Redoute (1817–1824), which was drawn up at the insistence of Josephine Beauharnais, wife of Napoleon I. It depicts from nature the collections of roses in the castle of Malmaison. The known varieties at that time numbered about 250.

According to Harvey, roses may be classified in the following way: hybrid teas, with large, individual flowers having several petals of varied colour, often fragrant, recurrently blooming, that are undoubtedly the most popular types of rose bush for the home gardener; floribundas (formerly called polyanthus), with semi-double or double flowers in clusters, hardy, floriferous, and long-lasting, among the most grown types; dwarf polyanthus, with a compact inflorescence and smaller flowers, suitable for edging; grandi-

133

134

135

floras, similar to floribundas but taller and with singly borne and clustered flowers on the same plant; shrub roses, comprising such ancient forms as musk roses, centifolias, damask roses, etc., now little grown; climbing, derived from *Rosa Wichuraiana* and including kinds ascribable to hybrids of tea or floribunda roses; miniature roses, of small stature; tea roses, of warm, dry climates, not now often grown, single-flowered, with their own particular aroma.

Cultivation. Sites suited to the growing of roses are exposed to full sun or are only lightly shaded (floribundas are a little less exacting in regard to light). The soil may be variable but must always be well fertilized, and well drained. Planting is done in autumn or early spring. Often, to avoid moisture loss and to control weeds, the beds are mulched. Any suckers from the root-stock should be removed. In general, pruning is severe, just above a dormant leaf bud facing outwards, with a slanting cut, preferably before growth begins in spring. Stems injured by frost or disease and dead stems are removed, and flowering stems reduced to two leaf buds. With tree roses, care should be taken not to destroy the symmetry of the crown.

Other than for flowering beds and borders and for covering walls, arches, pergolas, and pillars in the open air, roses are grown for cut flowers. The latter bloom in the greenhouse out of season and the desired form is a single flower on a long stem, which is obtained by using hybrid tea varieties with a solitary flower, removing side buds if necessary.

In the garden the hybrid teas bloom in June-July and again in September, so a continuous succession of flowers can be obtained. Indeed, in some districts blooms can be had in December.

The propagation of roses is usually by budding on a hardy type. Older varieties and climbers may be propagated by cuttings.

Many troubles beset roses. Aphids attack the underside of the leaves, the new shoots, and the flower peduncle, causing the plant to weaken, and the leaves and flower buds to be misshapen. Thrips cause spotting of the leaves and deformation of the flower buds. These insects may be controlled with appropriate insecticides. The red mite, more dangerous in the greenhouse, makes leaves turn yellow and fall.

Among diseases, the most serious are powdery mildew and black spot, which may be kept in check by frequent fungicidal sprays.

Chlorosis of the leaves in calcareous soil is due to iron deficiency and may be corrected by spraying with chelated iron or with ferrous sulphate. In spite of these drawbacks, British gardeners produce roses of outstanding beauty.

130-135. The cultivars of roses are so numerous as to make cataloguing them difficult. Pictured here:

130 Nymph, a polyanthus rose.

131. Blaze.

132. Romantic.

133. Baccarat, a climber.

134. Bettina

135. Gail Borden.

136. *Wisteria floribunda* with violet flowers.

136

137

138

Wisteria

Wisteria floribunda, family Leguminosae
The genus is dedicated to Caspar Wistar, anatomist.

Morphology. This plant is a woody vine with deciduous, unequally pinnate leaves with oval-lanceolate leaflets, silky underneath when young. The stem is twisted into spirals and can reach considerable length; it has a brown-grey bark dotted with numerous lenticels, later slightly fissured. The branches are abundant and wrap themselves around any support, including the trunk.

The flowers are quite showy, butterfly-like, of a light violet blue, fragrant, and appear in spring in drooping, terminal racemes; sometimes they have a light flowering towards the end of summer. The pods are compressed, silky, and many-seeded.

Varieties. *Alba*, *rosea*, *variegata*, *macrobotrys*, and *violaceo-plena* with double flowers, are among the best known varieties.

Origin. This species is native to Japan. It tolerates cold, requires sun, is suited to any soil, and grows to 30 feet.

Cultivation. This is the most-used climber for covering trellises, walls, and pergolas, sometimes supporting them. It is a honey plant.

The varieties and cultivars are grafted on *Wisteria frutescens*, sometimes by root graft; it also is propagated by layering, stem cuttings, root cuttings and by seed. Another species, less widespread, is *W. sinensis*, native to China, with a smaller number of leaflets in the compound leaf and with scentless flowers.

Other species. Among climbing plants *Campsis radicans*, called trumpet vine, is popular for its large, tubular flowers, opening abruptly in five rounded, irregular lobes, orange outside, red inside. The climbing stems need no assistance since they have aerial rootlets. It is a hardy, sun-loving species, preferring cool soil, and is native to the U.S. It is propagated by cuttings or layering.

137. *Wisteria floribunda* var. alba.

138, 139. *Campis radicans* and detail of the corolla.

139

Golden-chain tree and broom

Genera *Laburnum* and *Cytisus*, family Leguminosae

This group of related genera has included in the past a number of classifications which are now grouped in the two genera. They were first introduced into Britain in the late sixteenth century.

The most interesting species is *Laburnum anagyroides* (= *Cytisus Laburnum*).

Morphology. This is a small tree 20 to 30 feet tall or, in cultivated forms, an erect, branching shrub. The branches are erect or spreading, pendulous at the tips; the bark is smooth; the leaves are large, trifoliate, dark green and smooth on top, lighter and hairy underneath.

The spring flowers, fragrant, in the characteristic pea-shape, are in long, terminal, pendulous racemes, a beautiful golden yellow with a purple spot on the standard; the fruit is a pod.

Cultivation. Golden-chain tree prefers a cool, well-drained soil, and full sun. It does well in shrubberies and can be trained over arches and pergolas. To ensure regular flowering it is advisable to remove seed pods after flowering; this also keeps the tree vigorous.

The wood is hard and close-grained, and is used for small articles. All parts of the plant (leaves, flowers, and especially the fruits) are poisonous.

Propagation is by seed in March or April, or by layering; varieties are usually grafted on the type species.

Other species. *Cytisus purpureus* is distinguished from other species by its purple-white or pink flowers. It is a small plant, to about 2 feet, native to the eastern Alps. It is sometimes grafted high on the *Laburnum* to give a specimen with a developed trunk.

Common broom (*Cytisus scoparius*) is a thickly branched shrub, with thin, green branches, almost devoid of leaves, with rather large golden flowers. It is adapted to most well-drained soils, and prefers full sun. It has many varieties, differing in flower colour. It is native to Europe and particularly Britain. Other countries refer to it as Scotch broom.

---

140. *Laburnum anagyroides* (Golden-Chain Tree).

141. *Cytisus sessilifolius.*

142. *Cytisus scoparius* (Scotch Broom).

Azaleas and rhododendrons

Genus *Rhododendron*, family Ericaceae
The rhododendrons constitute a group of ornamental plants of great importance. Azaleas and rhododendrons cannot be separated botanically, although many azaleas are deciduous. The hardy varieties of rhododendrons were introduced to Britain in the mid-eighteenth century.

Morphology. This genus includes at least 350 species, all woody plants, quite varied in size, form and flower colour, and including a great number of horticultural species. They are shrubs ranging from 1 to 60 feet, evergreen or deciduous, with alternate, entire leaves.

Flowers are borne on pedicels, in terminal umbel-like racemes; the flower is rotate, bell-shaped or funnel-shaped, most often with five lobes, white or in any shade of rose, red, violet, yellow, or orange; the fruit is a capsule containing numerous seeds.

Varieties. Bailey, the authority on horticulture, distinguishes between rhododendrons, deciduous azaleas and Indian azaleas.

Rhododendrons are those plants that enrich the shrubberies, gardens and parks with their superb, abundant spring bloom and are ornamental for the rest of the year with their shiny, full foliage; among these the hybrids are the most numerous, including combinations of the North American, Himalayan, Sikh, and Chinese species.

Cultivation. The great ornamental quality of rhododendrons—which are slow-growing—is evident whether they are used as isolated specimens or in great masses; the dwarf species are suited to rock gardens and cliff plantings. In any case, these plants prefer mild winters, ample water, a humid atmosphere, light shade, protection from the wind and snow, and a soil rich in humus, cool, moderately-acid, and well drained. If the soil is alkaline add sulphur, peat moss, and leaf mould. The roots are very shallow and the soil must not be cultivated.

The rhododendrons transplant easily, provided they are moved with a ball of earth. Seed may be sown in pots in a mixture of peat and sand and covered lightly with sand or damp sphagnum. They may be propagated by cuttings of almost mature wood, or by division. Hybrids are grafted in winter in a warm greenhouse, on root-stock of *Rhododendron catawbiense*.

The deciduous azaleas, also used outdoors, flower from April to June, according to type. The Indian types are evergreen but must be kept in the greenhouse in winter.

Several insects and disease attack azaleas and rhododendrons, but most may be easily controlled. The most common problem with azaleas is chlorosis that develops in soils insufficiently acid. This may be corrected by spraying the plant with a ferrous solution.

143-148. Rhododendrons and azaleas have a large number of cultivars. Both the flowers and the foliage are ornamental.

145

146

144

147

148

149

151

150

Forsythia

Genus *Forsythia*, family Oleaceae
This genus comprises three species widely grown for the beauty of their flowers; *Forsythia suspensa*, *F. viridissima*, and hybrid *F. intermedia*.

Morphology. *F. suspensa*, a shrub which can grow to about 10 feet tall, has deciduous leaves; many slender, flexible, drooping branches; opposite, ovate, serrated leaves, often tripartite; bell-shaped flowers grouped in clusters at the nodes, deeply four-parted, bright golden yellow. This fruit is a capsule with winged seeds. The branches take root when they come into contact with the soil. Variety *Fortunei* is more erect with arching branches, is more vigorous, and has sulphur-yellow flowers with twisted petals.

F. viridissima differs in having erect branches, greenish-yellow flowers, and leaves toothed above the middle.

F. intermedia often has tripartite leaves and flowers like those of the variety *Fortunei*. A distinguishing characteristic among the three species is in the branches, hollow between the nodes in *F. suspensa*. There is layered pulp in the other two species, absent in the nodes of *F. intermedia* and present in the nodes of *F. viridissima*. *F. intermedia* has an excellent variety, *spectabilis*, whose flowers are more numerous, more colourful and larger than any other of the genus.

Origin. Both *F. suspensa* and *F. viridissima* are native to China.

Cultivation. These are shrubs adapted to any type of soil if not too compact and dry; they prefer a south or west wall or a sheltered shrubbery. Forsythias are valued for their abundant, showy bloom along the whole branch, which appears early (from March to April), before the leaves. These plants may also be forced in the greenhouse. They are propagated by division in September, by cuttings, or layering. They should be pruned heavily just after flowering.

The foliage is not attacked by insects, but is infected by disease; a blistering of the stem, a root rot, and two kinds of wilt may be problems.

152

153

154

Viburnum

Genus *Viburnum*, family Caprifoliaceae
The name of the genus is the old Latin name.

Morphology. The viburnums comprise a large group of about 120 species having in common the following characteristics: leaves almost always deciduous, opposite, most often entire; small flowers in dense terminal panicles or umbel-like cymes; fruit a single-seeded drupe, often of a vivid colour.

The species most often grown in gardens for its bloom is the Snowball, (*Viburnum Opulus* var. *roseum*), named for the large spring inflorescence, which is spherical, formed only of sterile flowers, and of large size. The flowers are limited to the outer part of the inflorescence which is globular. The leaves are tri-lobed. The fruit is bright red; the leaves become purple in autumn. It is a deciduous variety.

Other species. Rather widespread in the Mediterranean region, most suitable for hedges, the Laurestinus (*Viburnum Tinus*) has leathery evergreen, oval, and shiny leaves and white or pinkish flowers in summer.

The common deciduous *V. Lantana*, or Wayfaring-Tree, is suited for rock gardens; it has white flowers. Fruit is red, turning black.

The *V. Rhytidophyllum* is evergreen and has long, dense, reticulate leaves, dark green and shiny on top, whitish and tomentose underneath, with white flowers.

Probably the most beautiful deciduous flowering viburnum is *V. Carlesii*, a native of Korea. It is a shrub with numerous stiff branches, about 4 feet tall, with a down of stellate hairs on the young branches and on both sides of the leaves. The leaves are ovate, acute, and irregularly toothed. The flowers are clustered in semiglobular cymes, rose-coloured or white, and fragrant.

Cultivation. With the exception of the snowball and *V. Lantana*, all the viburnums prefer a cool soil and semi-shade. Dry positions should be avoided, and older specimens must not be overcrowded. Weak shoots must be removed in winter.

The viburnums are grown as isolated specimens, in clumps and in hedges for their flowers, their coloured fruit, and their foliage. Propagation is by seed after stratification. The evergreen kinds may be propagated by softwood cuttings in summer under glass, half-ripened shoots being inserted in sandy loam in gentle bottom heat in July and August. All may be propagated by division. The varieties with sterile flowers are grafted on *V. Opulus* or *V. Lantana* or propagated by cuttings.

149, 151. *Forsythia intermedia* in flower.

150. *Chaenomeles lagenaria* cultivar Rowallane (Japanese Flowering Quince).

152. Inflorescence of a viburnum.

153. Inflorescence of *Viburnum Carlesii*.

154. Fruit of *Viburnum Opulus*.

Foliage shrubs

Pittosporum

Pittosporum Tobira, family Pittosporaceae
The name of the genus comes from the Greek, meaning "resinous seed", it being covered with a sticky substance; *Tobira* is the Japanese name of this species.

Morphology. This is an evergreen shrub or small tree, which reaches a height of about 10 feet, with a twisted trunk covered with a smooth bark, having a globular form, with obovate, obtuse leaves narrowing to a wedge on a short petiole. The leaves are dense and leathery, smooth, dark green and shiny on top; their edges are entire and down-curved; leaves are alternate, appearing in whorls on the twigs.

The small flowers are white or greenish, with a strong fragrance resembling orange blossoms, in terminal panicles and appearing during winter in the south, or in spring. The fruits are ovoid capsules densely covered with short hairs. The variety *variegata* has leaves variegated with white.

Origin. This plant is native to China and Japan.

Cultivation. In Europe this shrub is widely grown along the Mediterranean coast, to whose climate it adapts because it tolerates summer drought and thrives on mild winters and is resistant to winds carrying salt spray. In Britain

155

156

157

it can be grown in the open in the warmest maritime regions of the south-west. In less favoured zones it must be planted in the shelter of a wall and in a warm spot. It needs acid soil.

For greenhouse culture it should be potted March or April, and kept at 60° to 70°F until October and from 40° to 50°F until April. It is valued for the ornamental foliage and the fragrance of the flowers, as well as for its vigour.

Pittosporum can be propagated by seed, which is, however, difficult to preserve. Seed is sown in a cool greenhouse in spring. Cuttings of half-mature wood up to 3 inches long may be planted in small pots of sandy soil, under bell-glass at a temperature of around 60°F, in summer.

Other species. Other species sometimes culti-vated, mostly native to Oceania, are *P. crassi-folium* (Karo) and *P. tenuifolium* (Tawhiwhi) from New Zealand, with dark purple flowers; *P. erioloma* and *P. viridiflorum* are similar to *P. Tobira*; *P. undulatum* (Victorian Box), native to Australia, is sometimes used as the stock for grafting.

---

155. *Pittosporum Tobira* in a Mediterranean garden.

156, 157. *Pittosporum Tobira* in flower, and detail.

158. Inflorescence of *Prunus Laurocerasus*.

159. High hedge of *Prunus Laurocerasus*.

158

159

Cherry laurel

Prunus Laurocerasus, family Rosaceae
Laurocerasus indicates that the fruit somewhat resembles cherries while the evergreen leaves may be likened to those of the laurel.

Morphology. This is an evergreen shrub or small tree growing to 20 feet, with an irregular crown; smooth grey bark; leaves obovate or elliptical with a pointed tip, on a short petiole, thick and leathery, with almost entire edges, shiny dark green on top, dull, and lighter green beneath.

The flowers, small and white, open in the spring in erect racemes that are terminal or axillary to the leaves and have a pleasing odour of bitter almonds. The inedible fruit is ovoid, small, fleshy, purple; leaves are poisonous.

Varieties. The botanical varieties are numerous and differ principally in the form and size of the leaves; those with large leaves come from the Caucasus, those with small leaves from the Balkans. The variety *Caucasica* is a fine, large-leaved form; *schipkaensis* has a pyramidal habit and is very hardy; *magnoliaefolia* has leaves up to 12 inches long similar to those of the magnolia; *rotundifolia* leaves are short and obtuse, a good hedging variety.

Origin. In nature this plant lives in cool areas; it is considered, like box, a species of Tertiary origin, at one time spread through other parts of Europe, as fossil remains show, and driven back to the places where it is found naturally today by Quaternary glaciers.

Cultivation. The cherry laurel is frequently employed for high hedges, fences, and espaliers which may be moderately pruned; it also adapts to planting in tubs for indoor use. It is propagated by cuttings of mature wood inserted in sheltered borders or cold frames in autumn. New varieties are grown by seeds. Pruning to shorten straggly growths is done in April.

Other species. A somewhat related species is *P. lusitanica* (Portugal Laurel) of the Iberian penin-sula and the Canary Islands, useful for hedging, with shiny, persistent leaves, and its varieties *azorica* with large leaves and *variegata* with leaves margined silver. A lesser known variety is *myrtifolia* that is notable for its dense form.

Holly

Ilex Aquifolium, family Aquifoliaceae

Morphology. The Common holly is a true tree, although cultivated specimens are for the most part bushy. The crown is dense with leathery, evergreen leaves dark and shiny on top, dull and lighter on the underside, ovate, mostly with coarse spiny teeth.

The flowers are small, white or somewhat pink, in axillary cymes on last year's growth; the plant is ordinarily dioecious; the fruits are shiny red berries. It is native to Europe, particularly Britain.

Varieties. *Heterophylla* has leaves entire; *pendula* has pendulous branches; *pyramidalis* is an excellent variety for berries; *variegata* has leaves mottled with silver and gold; *ferox* (Hedgehog Holly) is prickly also on the top side of the leaf; *bacciflava* has yellow berries.

Cultivation. Holly prefers a cool, humid climate and acid soil. It is suitable for hedges since it is easy to shape, and the berries persist part of the winter.

Holly is propagated by seeds stratified after the fleshy portion is removed; the varieties are propagated by grafting or by cuttings of mature wood. This method serves to ensure that female plants will be obtained. When transplanting, it should be moved with a root ball.

Other species. *I. opaca* is the native American holly. *I. crenata* is the Japanese holly; *I. cornuta* is the Chinese holly. Greenhouse species cultivated include *I. Cassine* native to America, and *paraguariensis*, "Paraguay Tea" from Brazil. *Euonymous japonicus* belongs to a related family (Celastraceae). It is evergreen, spreading, with oval, shiny leaves, edged with small, obscure teeth, in some varieties marbled or edged with golden yellow. Frequently used in borders is the evergreen *Aucuba japonica*, often with marbled yellow leaves tolerant of shade.

160, 162. *Ilex Aquifolium* in a form with marginate leaves.

161. Berries of *Ilex Aquifolium*.

163. *Aucuba japonica*.

164. *Euonymus japonicus* with variegated foliage.

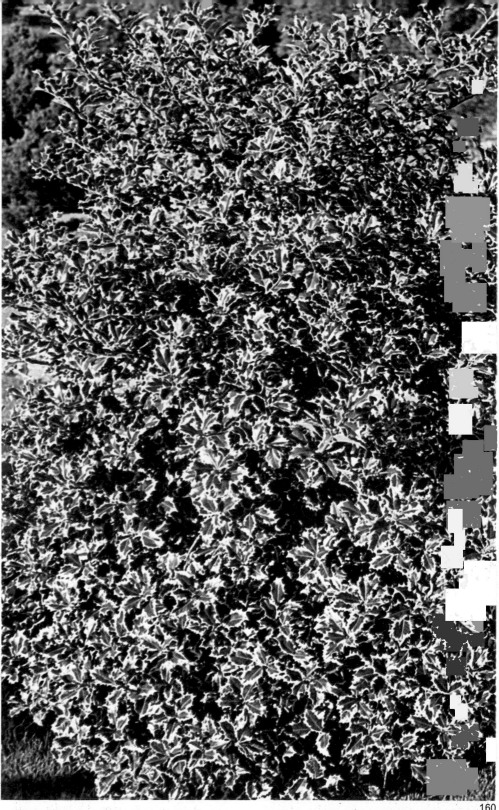

160

161

162

163

164

165

166

Box

Buxus sempervirens, family Buxaceae
The genus name was in use among the early Romans. *Sempervirens* means "evergreen".

Morphology. This is a hardy evergreen shrub with small stiff leaves, at the most 20 feet tall, but along the Black and Caspian seas it becomes a true tree. The trunk is covered with light, scaly bark; leaves are dense, small, oval, opposite, entire, almost sessile, leathery, dark green and shiny on top.

The spring flowers are yellowish, small, grouped in axillary clusters. The fruit is a capsule. The presence of alkaloids makes box a poisonous plant, and no part of it should be eaten.

Varieties. The most widely cultivated species are *B. balearica* native to the Balearic Islands, 8 feet; and *B. sempervirens* varieties such as *argenteo-variegata*, *angustifolia*, *marginata*, *glauca*, *rotundifolia*, *rosmarinifolia*, *myrtifolia* (dwarf with narrow leaves), and *bullata* (with bulbous leaves). *B. microphylla*, 3 feet, is native to Japan, and its variety *japonica* has various forms.

Origin. Box is native to the chains of the Atlas Mountains, and European regions with a Mediterranean, sub-Mediterranean, or Atlantic climate; usually it occurs in rocky areas or in shady undergrowth. It is not associated with any particular soil but is usually found in limestone soils in Europe. *B. microphylla* is usually found in acid soils in Japan. All varieties are slow growing, although some grow more rapidly than others.

Cultivation. Box is used to make dense hedges that may be pruned to any form, and the dwarf varieties are used for edging. It is valued for its adaptability to shade. It is drought-resistant and should always be in well-drained soil.

---

165. Detail of *Buxus sempervirens*.

166. *Buxus balearica*.

Privet

Ligustrum ovalifolium, family Oleaceae
The name of the genus is an ancient Latin term; that of the species indicates the leaf form.

Morphology. This privet is a large semi-evergreen shrub or small tree extending up to 15 feet tall, with smooth, opposite, ovalelliptical, thick, entire, dark green leaves, shiny on top, sometimes purple in autumn.

The small white flowers appear in June or July, have four petals, are in panicles and have a strong fragrance; the fruit are blackberry-like drupes.

Varieties. Of cultivated varieties, the following are interesting: *aureo-marginatum* (leaves edged with yellow), *variegatum* (with yellow-marbled leaves), *tricolor* (leaves variegated white and yellowish, pink when young), *multiflorum* (flowering abundantly), and *lucidum* with broad, lustrous foliage that grows to 18 feet.

Origin. This species is native to Japan. It may be planted in any soil. It is of no great ornamental value.

Because privet is chiefly used for hedging in Britain it has become susceptible to a number of root diseases including white root rot which is usually confined to the south-west of England. In the north of England a fungi *Verticullum dahliae* has been found on the roots of privet. Dieback and canker of privet twigs has been reported as being caused by *Glomerella cingulata* which is responsible for Bitter rot of apples.

Cultivation. It tolerates drought, salt, and a certain amount of shade. It grows rapidly. It is used to create hedges (it may be pruned to any shape), as centres of flower beds, and as single specimens. Propagation is by hardwood or softwood cuttings, by division or by seed. Varieties are grafted on the type species. Cuttings should be about 9 to 12 inches in length, planted outdoors from late August to November in a shady position.

Other species. A related species also grown for hedges is *Ligustrum vulgare* (common privet), widespread in Britain, distinguishable by its smaller leaves, deciduous and less pointed, and by its small stature. It is hardier than *L. ovalifolium*. This privet also has many varieties, including *buxifolium* (semipersistent, obtuse leaves), *glaucum* (leaves edged in white), *atrovirens* (with narrow leaves, almost persistent), *pendulum*, *pyramidale* (habit pyramidal), *chlorocarpum*, *leucocarpum*, *xanthocarpum* (respectively with greenish, white, and yellow fruit), *aureum* (leaves yellow), and others.

---

167. Inflorescence of *Ligustrum ovalifolium*.

168. Privet pruned to ornamental shapes.

169. A species of pyracantha with yellow fruit.

170. A form of pyracantha with orange fruit.

171. Detail of *Pyracantha coccinea*.

172. *Crataegus Oxyacantha* var. *coccinea*.

167

168

Fruiting shrubs

Pyracantha

Pyracantha coccinea, family Rosaceae
The generic name derives from the Greek words *pyr*, "fire", and *acantha*, "thorn". *Coccineus*, in Latin, means "red". The common name is "firethorn".

Morphology. This is a handsome evergreen shrub up to 20 feet tall, with small, alternate, oval-oblong leaves, shallowly-toothed or in some cases entire, stipulate, thick, and shiny green. The branches are spiny.

The flowers are small, white, and numerous in corymbs during May and June; fruits are small round pomes in red, orange, or yellow.

Varieties. The variety *Lalandii* is hardier and has broader clusters and orange-rose fruits; *crenulata*, Nepalese White Thorn, grows up to 15 feet and needs wall protection; its variety *Rogersiana* has glossy foliage and orange fruits.

Origin. The shrub is native to Southern Europe and Asia Minor. The variety *Lalandii* comes from central and western China.

Cultivation. It prefers a well-drained soil and thrives on acid or limestone soil. It is propagated by seed, by cuttings of mature wood kept in a moderately warm greenhouse, by division, and sometimes by grafting on hawthorn or cotoneaster.

It is well adapted to rocky slopes and to shrub borders and makes an excellent hedge.

Other species. Other cultivated kinds are *Pyracantha crenato-serrata* with coral-red fruit, native to China, and *P. angustifolia*, also from China, with narrow leaves and orange fruit.

169

171

170

172

173

Cotoneaster

Genus *Cotoneaster*, family Rosaceae

Morphology. These are shrubs or, rarely, small trees, devoid of spines. They are deciduous or evergreen, with entire leaves.

The flowers are small, borne singly or in terminal cymes, white or pink, with five petals; the fruit is small, spherical, often red.

Species and varieties. The Chinese *Cotoneaster bullata* is a spreading bush, with few branches, growing to 6 feet. Leaves are rather large, deciduous, ovate, greyish-green underneath. The pinkish flowers appear in May and June and the fruits are bright red. The varieties *floribunda* and *macrophylla*, abundantly flowered, are very handsome.

C. acutifolia from Central China is a shrub of vigorous growth up to 10 feet with black fruit. Its variety *villosula* has leaves pubescent underneath.

C. Dielsiana, also from China, is a shrub growing up to 6 feet tall, with spreading and arching branches and small, deciduous, ovate to elliptical leaves and red fruit. The variety *elegans* has smaller, semipersistent leaves.

C. horizontalis is prostrate, with distichous branches covering the ground; in autumn the leaves turn yellow first, then red, falling off the shrub quite late; the abundant fruits are ovoid and red. The variety *perpusilla* has very small leaves.

C. Conspicua var. *decora* is another prostrate form bearing many berries.

Also native to China, *C. salicifolia* is evergreen or nearly so, up to 15 feet tall, with elliptical-oblong to ovate-lanceolate leaves that are acute, rough, and glabrous on top; the fruit is a bright red.

C. integerrima, suited to rock gardens, has deciduous foliage, downy underneath, and red fruits. *C. microphylla*, 2 feet, trailing is suitable for walls and rockeries. *C. tomentosa* with obtuse leaves is native to Europe and is particularly adapted to limestone soils. Since hybridization is easy in this genus, numerous hardy cultivars have been developed, with coloured autumn foliage.

C. Watereri is a vigorous free-fruiting hybrid, growing to 15 feet. *Zabelii* with purple pear-shaped berries, originating in China, grows to 6 feet.

Cultivation. The cotoneasters prefer well-drained soil and full sun. They are at their best as colour highlights and, especially in their prostrate forms, adorning rock gardens. The fruit, persisting part of the winter, is rather decorative. Propagation is by seed sown 1 inch deep outdoors in March. The evergreen species may be propagated by cuttings of half-mature wood inserted in sandy soil in frames in September, and by grafting on *C. integerrima*, and by division.

---

173. A cotoneaster, with fruit.

174. *Cotoneaster integerrima.*